Disney

THE MUPPETS

CHARACTER ENCYCLOPEDIA

DISNEY

THE MUPPETS

CHARACTER ENCYCLOPEDIA

Written by
Craig Shemin

MUPPET LABS
SEAL OF APPROVAL

To ensure your enjoyment and safety, this book has been researched, tested and scientifically examined at the molecular level. Muppet Labs has given its prestigious seal of approval, which means the book is guaranteed to not spontaneously turn you upside down or topsy-turvy. As far as anything else is concerned: you're on your own.

Contents

Introduction

Hi-ho and welcome to the first ever official Muppets Character Encyclopedia!

Ever since I sat in the swamp and first dreamed of a life in show business, I always hoped that I wouldn't be alone in my journey.

As I moved through my career from the swamp to local television, *The Muppet Show*, and the movies, I've collected a troupe of lovable crazies—pigs and bears and whatevers who share my dream of "singing and dancing and making people happy." I call them my friends. You call them the Muppets.

This book features many of my Muppet friends, but there wasn't enough room for everyone. To the cows, horses, lions, tigers, bears, and assorted unidentifiable creatures who couldn't make it: I apologize. To the Muppet monsters who aren't here: I'm asking you nicely—please don't eat me.

There was one other friend we couldn't put in the encyclopedia—YOU! Y'see, we consider you folks in the audience to be a big part of the Muppets. We couldn't do it without you (or to be more exact, we wouldn't do it without you). So as you leaf through the book, imagine yourself right there alongside your favorite Muppet. Thanks for being part of our family.

Enjoy!

Kermit the Frog™

LOVELY INTRO, KERMIE, BUT YOU DIDN'T MENTION MOI ONCE!

Afghan Hound

Full-fledged member

of the O.M.D. (Organization of Muppet Dogs), Afghan Hound enjoys performing in sketches, as well as chasing cars and her own tail. Although she tells everyone she's a pedigree pooch, the only papers she's ever had are the ones in her litter tray.

DOES YOUR DOG HAVE A LICENSE?

LICENSE? HE DOESN'T EVEN KNOW HOW TO DRIVE!

Star Performer

With her shiny coat and bright eyes, Afghan stands out in ensemble production numbers, like "Upidee" in *The Muppet Show*.

Hungry Hound

Afghan appeared in the 2011 film, *The Muppets*. While manning the phones during the Muppet Telethon, Afghan used her off time to order a pizza. The cliffhanger of the movie was whether or not the pizza was delivered.

LARGE PIZZA, PLEASE!

Cold nose, warm heart

The first trick Afghan ever learned was dialing long distance.

MUPPET FILE

Debut The Muppet Show #214
Talents Singing, dancing, sitting, staying, scratching fleas
Dislikes Flea and tick season

12

Andy and Randy

Miss Piggy's nephews Andy and Randy started out at the Muppets' TV station, K-MUP, with a little help from their famous aunt. Andy and Randy consistently delivered the kind of work that gives favoritism a bad name.

Eager Pigs

What Andy and Randy lack in brain power, they make up for in enthusiasm and an amazing ability to cause mayhem. They recently tried to start a business, but, unfortunately for them, self-serve nuclear fuel has limited appeal.

MUPPET FILE

Debut Muppet Classic Theater

I.Q. Barely

Favorite food Yes, please!

This Little Piggy

In the Muppet version of the Three Little Pigs, Andy and Randy portrayed Miss Piggy's brothers. Miss Piggy was not amused even though she quite liked being called "little" for once.

Undersized craniums

BAD GENES...

GOOD JEANS!

Sam and Friends

Kermit the Frog got his start in show business on a local Washington, D.C. television program named *Sam and Friends*. The five-minute show featured Kermit and the earliest Muppet performers acting in short sketches and lip-synching along with pop songs.

Kermit always dresses for an important occasion.

Wearing shades inside? They don't call him Harry the Hipster for nothing.

I ALWAYS WONDERED WHERE KERMIT WENT.

Sam thinks he is starting to lose his hair.

Together Again
Reunited for the Muppets' 30th anniversary special, the friends picked up right where they had left off. Sam remained silent, Harry was as hip as ever, and Yorick still ate everything in sight.

Yorick is getting impatient for dinner.

Angel Marie

After hundreds of unsuccessful attempts at auditioning for leading roles, Angel Marie broke through playing a pirate in *Muppet Treasure Island*. To prepare for the role, he stopped bathing for a month—and he has yet to resume.

Nip/Tuck
Like many performers, Angel Marie has undergone cosmetic surgery. We would have shown you the before picture, but it self-destructed.

ARRRRRRRH!

Stunt Man
In *Muppet Treasure Island*, Angel Marie did all his own stunts (and ate his own lunch).

Angel Marie wears incredibly large contact lenses.

MUPPET FILE

Debut *Muppet Treasure Island*

Training Miss Diana's Charm School & Truck Stop

Favorite Movies *Pirates of the Caribbean* and *Bambi*

Learned to give himself stitches from the how-to book *Suture Self*.

Angus McGonagle

As a child, Angus McGonagle gained a gift of gargle and a love of the music of George Gershwin. His stirring performance of "Summertime" brings tears to audiences' eyes and a knot to his throat.

> I LOVE IT WHEN THE MUPPETS PLAY GERSHWIN.

> TOO BAD GERSHWIN ALWAYS LOSES.

> I GARGLE GERSHWIN... GORGEOUSLY!

Big Break Broken
Angus's big chance at fame as a guest on *The Muppet Show* was interrupted by the unexpected arrival of Luke Skywalker, C-3PO, R2-D2, and Chewbacca of *Star Wars*.

Musical gargling is all in the tongue.

Bonnie Lad
Angus's unique talents were discovered by Kermit the Frog, who booked him on *The Muppet Show*. Kermit was looking for a unique interpretation of Gershwin.

What does a gargoyle wear under his kilt? Whatever he wants to!

MUPPET FILE
Debut *The Muppet Show* #417
Species Gargoyle
Favorite Song "Summertime"

Animal

The Electric Mayhem band's passionate percussionist is known for his love of music, the ladies, and his hunger for everything else. No one knows exactly where Animal came from (or where he goes at night), and it's probably better that way.

Raising the Roof
An encounter with Muppet Labs' Insta-Grow pills makes Animal grow to enormous size. But luckily for everyone, the effects were only temporary.

Anger Management
Animal's retirement from playing the drums and entry into anger management lasted a short time. A tiny angel and devil argued over Animal's return to music—they were the only ones who ever dared to get that close to him.

Animal combed his fur once in 1978.

Secret Softie
Animal may be unpredictable and short-tempered, but he does have a softer side. This is revealed if you engage him in a discussion of his beloved momma or fluffy bunny rabbits.

MUPPET FILE
Debut
The Muppet Show pilot
Likes Meditation, collecting stamps, and bunny rabbits
Species
Unknown

Annie Sue

Actress Annie Sue may be younger, prettier, and more talented than Miss Piggy, but she lacks Miss Piggy's unique star quality (and her expertise in karate). However, Annie is a happy and enthusiastic performer and she greets everyone (even Miss Piggy) with a smile.

YEAH. HOW DID SHE END UP WITH THE MUPPETS?

THAT PIG IS ACTUALLY VERY TALENTED.

Perm was once temporary. And now it's not.

Rumors of a nose job have never been proven.

In Demand
Annie Sue has spent her recent years on stage in such shows as "Sow Pacific," "The Pigs of Penzance," and "Mary Porkins." Annie Sue rejoined her friends (and Miss Piggy) for *Muppets Most Wanted*.

Pig vs. Pig
Miss Piggy always considered herself the divine swine of The Muppet Theater, so when Annie Sue, a younger, more talented pig showed up, there was friction. But Annie is not one to make trouble—she just wants to perform.

MUPPET FILE
Debut *The Muppet Show* #214
Species Pig
Special Talents Anything Piggy can do, Annie Sue can do better

Baskerville

There are lots of dogs in the Muppet family—and with good reason. They're loyal, obedient, and they learn their lines quickly. Baskerville is no exception. He may not be "Best in Show," but this reliable pooch puts on a doggone good performance.

Unlucky Hound
Baskerville once played Dr. Watson in a Sherlock Holmes sketch. He was eaten by the suspect before Sherlock Rowlf solved the mystery.

Commercial Success
Baskerville and Rowlf were originally on TV commercials and reunited for several appearances on *The Muppet Show*. They have little bark, no bite, but brother, they can belt out a tune!

Versatile Performer
A faithful member of the Muppet ensemble, Baskerville is equally at home in songs, sketches, and veterinarians' offices. He is currently writing his memoirs, *Tails From My Youth*.

Baskerville has his ears fluffed every three months.

Wears a lucky flea collar under his bow. (Not so lucky for the fleas.)

MUPPET FILE
Debut Purina Dog Food Commercial

Likes Howling at the moon

Favorite Food Asparagus

Beaker

When he was training for a life in science, Beaker never dreamed he would be involved in so many breakthroughs. He has broken through walls, floors, and ceilings. Squeaky-voiced Beaker has learned that science is hard—as are most of the surfaces in Muppet Labs.

Hair mousse mixed with car wax

Send in the Clones
A mishap with a copy machine in the Muppet Labs once caused the Muppet Theater to be filled with copies of Beaker. This made Bunsen nearly as nervous as Beaker.

Guinea Pig
Beaker is the dutiful but anxious assistant to Muppet Labs' chief scientist Dr. Bunsen Honeydew. He has helped to test countless inventions, and tested the limits of his own medical knowlege!

Banana Drama
The Banana Sharpener is just one of hundreds of Muppet Labs innovations. In this experiment, Beaker narrowly avoided being impaled by his recommended daily requirement of potassium.

Does not bite his nails. He doesn't have any.

MUPPET FILE

Debut *The Muppet Show* #202

Education B.S. in Pain Mismanagement from Hurt U.

Awards Webby Award for his performance of "Ode to Joy"

Bean Bunny

Bean Bunny is the Muppets' own "D.C.C."—Designated Cute Character. When Kermit and the gang tired of being cute, they called in Bean to take some of the responsibility. He is energetic, eager to please, and annoyingly adorable.

Cutesy Capers

Bean has had featured roles in *The Muppet Christmas Carol* and in Jim Henson's Muppet*Vision 3D attraction at Disney parks in Florida and California. He also works part time as a Cuteness Consultant for children's pageants.

Bunny Business

Bean grew up in a quiet meadow, but, like Kermit before him, he left home to pursue a career in show business in the big city.

Bean practices this innocent look in the mirror for hours.

A Tough Role

Bean hoped to break out of his adorable image by playing a weapon-toting action hero in the adventure *Beanbo*. Sadly, the entire budget was spent making the trailer.

I'M CUTE!

MUPPET FILE

Debut *The Tale of the Bunny Picnic*

Cuteness Rating Off the chart

Likes Everybody and everything . . . ever

24

Beauregard

The janitor and chief stagehand at The Muppet Theater, Beauregard is known for his strength of body and weakness of mind. In addition to his full time job, Beau has been known to pick up some extra cash as a taxi driver. He hopes to someday get a driver's license.

All Aboard!
In *Muppets Most Wanted*, Beauregard plays a conductor on an exciting European rail tour. Unfortunately, his Mop couldn't get a visa and had to stay home. Beau promised to send postcards.

Beau likes wooden-handled mops best.

Backstage Sage
Beau visited Veterinarian's Hospital when he was convinced the world was going to end. They made him pay his bill in advance—just in case it did.

Favorite plaid shirt. Beau calls it "Harry."

THE HEAVIER THE BETTER!

Handy Muppet
Need something heavy to be moved? Call Beauregard—that's his specialty. He can also move light things, but doesn't enjoy it as much.

MUPPET FILE
Debut
The Muppet Show #310

Special Talent
Lifting things

Favorite Possession
His mop

Beautiful Day

At the urging of his mother, Beautiful Day attended law school and became an attorney. But, after eating a judge during a particularly difficult trial, he decided to pursue a career where his talent for devouring his peers could be truly appreciated— show business.

Flat Man
In one of his featured roles in *The Muppet Show*, Beautiful Day gave a very two-dimensional performance. He was later re-inflated with a bicycle pump.

What's in a Name?
Beautiful Day was named after an interaction he had with a little girl who expressed joy over a beautiful day. The careless monster managed to ruin it for her.

SNARR RATCH CRUNDREDGE!

The Return of BD
Beautiful Day took a leave of absence to pursue a career in floral arranging, but he recently returned with appearances in several projects, including *The Muppets*.

Loose-fitting fur allows for expansion when he eats.

Uses special anti-dandruff monster shampoo to keep his fur fluffy.

MUPPET FILE
Debut *The Ed Sullivan Show*
Likes Very little
Dislikes Days ending in "Y"

Behemoth

> HE'S THE BEST! HE'S BRILLIANT! WHAT A PERFORMER!

> GOOD THINKING. HE ATE THE LAST CRITIC WHO GAVE HIM A BAD REVIEW.

A youngest child, Behemoth was expected to join the family's aluminum siding business, but he decided to go into show business, taking on the unassuming stage name Behemoth. In recent years, some of his co-workers have begun calling Behemoth by his real name, Gene.

Smashing Habit

In his spare time when not taking to stage or screen, Behemoth likes to collect pretty commemorative plates... then smashes them.

Behemoth is a natural blonde.

Open Wide

It's a good thing Behemoth smiled for this picture or no one would have noticed he accidentally ate Pepe. He couldn't resist Pepe's cologne—Eau de Garlic.

> HI. YOU SURE GOT NICE TEETH.

Voted "Most Likely to Eat a Classmate" in high school.

MUPPET FILE

Debut
The Muppet Show #114

Favorite Song "I've Got You Under My Skin"

Pet Peeve Getting gum in his fur

Big Mean Carl

When he was little, Carl had one wish—to be big. A chance encounter with a carnival fortune telling machine ended with Carl eating it. His wish hasn't come true yet. He wanted to be as big as his brother... his really big brother!

Consistent Performer
Carl is a performer with great range. But his big finish is always the same. (Hint: Someone gets eaten... and it's not Carl.)

Bohemian Rat-sody
After Carl ate Rizzo and two other rats during "Bohemian Rhapsody," the rats now refuse to appear with Carl unless he has a big breakfast first and is on a vermin-free diet.

Live and Let Diet
Carl and Clifford forged a pact during production of *Muppets Tonight*. Carl agreed not to eat Clifford as long as Clifford agreed to stop looking so tasty.

Carl's doctor once told him to "open wide" and was never seen again.

MUPPET FILE
Debut Muppet Meeting Films

Likes Anything—with salt

Special Talent Digestion

THANK YOU!

28

Bill the Bubble Guy

When it comes to unique talents and abilities, few performers come close to Bill the Bubble Guy: He makes bubbles come out of his head. When he was Bill the Bubble Baby, he entertained the other children for hours on end.

Living in a Bubble
With a gift like his, Bill was destined for a life in show business. After a brief stint in the special effects department, he was given a chance to perform.

Bubble dispenser positioned on top of Bill's head

Soapy Showman
Though his act is limited, he perseveres in show business and moonlights as a hat cleaner. Bill also is available for children's parties and Bar Mitzvahs.

> I'M BILL. I MAKE BUBBLES COME OUT OF MY HEAD.

Working Clean
Bill's squeaky clean act makes him a favorite of network executives looking for suitable material. His specialty is soap operas.

Suit purchased from Manny's House of Plaid and Seersucker

MUPPET FILE
Debut *Muppets Tonight* #105
Favorite Song "I'm Forever Blowing Bubbles"
Favorite pastime Bubble baths

Muppets Hit The Road

In *Muppets Most Wanted*, the whole gang embarks on a European tour via an international railway journey. Considering that one time they went to Europe, they flew in the cargo hold of an airplane, this isn't a bad way to travel.

Birds

Many different bird species are part of the Muppet family. This page represents all of the proud members of the bird family not represented elsewhere in the book and is included at the urging of their agent.

MUPPET FILE
Debut Various
Like Cats (the musical)
Dislike Cats (the animals)

Betsy Bird
A master of eccentric dance, Betsy Bird trained at the Avian Alley School of Dance. She has taken some time off from her career to feather her nest and raise a family.

Birds of a Feather
Not only do birds of a feather flock together, they perform together too. Piano legend Liberace once played a musical tribute to Muppet birds.

Gawky Birds
At almost 11ft (3 meters) tall, the Gawky birds are among the tallest birds in the world, and one of the few species who appear in variety show musical numbers.

Bright red head plumage to attract attention.

Understated head plumage to blend in.

No head plumage, but he's saving up for a wig.

Bobby Benson's Baby Band

Music in its infancy

Bobby Benson is the conductor and guardian of the baby band that bears his name. He won the contract of the baby band in a poker game and has handled their business affairs, musical arrangements, and diaper changes ever since.

Baby, One More Time
There are six members of the baby band and as the babies grow up, they're quickly replaced. To date, there have been about 1,489 former members of Bobby Benson's Baby Band, many of whom have gone into politics.

Bad Habits
Although he's had some bad times (including an arrest for an unspecified charge involving lemon meringue in the late 1970s), Bobby seems to have cleaned up his act.

Always wears shades even though his future's not so bright.

In Demand
Bobby and the babies cancelled a booking at the Lollapalooza festival to make an appearance in *The Muppets*. They've played to standing-room-only audiences at major concert venues, and crawling-room-only audiences at major day care centers.

THAT'S MY BABIES!

MUPPET FILE
Debut The Muppet Show #319
Training (Bobby) School of Hard Knocks
Training (Babies) Julliard Day Care Academy

Bobo

Bobo first joined the Muppets as a security guard, however his lovable personality (and the fact that robberies at the studio increased with Bobo on the job) led Kermit to give the bear a chance in front of the camera.

Pampered Bear
Bobo keeps clean by following a regimen of using specially formulated shampoo, but once got stuck for three days in a lather/rinse/repeat cycle.

Faking Bad
In movies like *The Muppets* and *Muppets from Space*, Bobo tends to play goofy henchmen to the bad guys. But, he's just acting—he doesn't even know how to spell "henchmen."

Home Sleep Home
Bobo hails from the woods of Pennsylvania. He wants to return home at hibernation time, but he keeps sleeping through it.

He's the Muppet bear who doesn't always wear a hat.

Told he has his mother's eyes, Bobo doesn't understand why he can't see what she does.

OOOOKAY, SIR.

MUPPET FILE
Debut
Muppets Tonight #101
Special Talents Bathing
Favorite Food
Food

Bossmen

DON'T YOU THINK THE BOSSMEN ARE TALENTED?

Welcome to the stage, the Bossmen! A rare species of feathered, wingless bird-like creatures, the Bossmen have an appreciation for music and an innate dancing ability. The gigantic jivers just have to feel the beat and their limbs do the rest.

BOSSMEN? I THOUGHT THOSE WERE GIANT FEATHER DUSTERS!

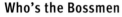

Who's the Bossmen
The Bossmen have smaller counterparts —Small Bossmen. They may be smaller, but they are the brains of the operation—the real boss men of the Bossmen.

I DIG THAT CRAZY BEAT!

The Bossmen have gangly, spaghetti-like limbs.

Their kneecaps are the Bossmen's most ticklish area.

Can experience a fear of heights while just standing.

Vegas, Baby!
The big guys first performed in Nancy Sinatra's Las Vegas act, to the song "Big Boss Man"—that's how they got their name. While their exact origins remain a mystery, the Bossmen continue to appear with the Muppets from time to time. When not dancing, they moonlight as chimney sweeps.

MUPPET FILE
Debut
Nancy Sinatra's Live Las Vegas Act

Special Talents
Taking very large steps

Dislikes Doorways and low-hanging studio lights

Brewster

The wise old man of the Muppets, Brewster has dedicated his time to discovering the meaning of life and how they get the lead inside of pencils. Brewster spent several years atop one of the Andes Mountains. He wasn't enjoying nature or seeking guidance—he just took a wrong turn.

Twinkle Toes
For an older gentleman, Brewster appeared light on his feet in "At the Dance". He appeared that way because he was standing on his partner's feet.

Tiring Job
Brewster spends his days dozing off and occasionally meditating, often falling into a deep sleep. He takes lots of breaks for food and to catch up on his favorite soap opera.

First runner-up for best eyebrows at a Facial Hair Festival

Can't tell where his hair stops and his beard begins.

WE HAVE A SAYING IN MY COUNTRY... I WISH I COULD REMEMBER WHAT IT IS.

MUPPET FILE
Debut *The Muppets Valentine Show* pilot

Special Talents Pondering

Favorite Chair Whichever one he is in

Bunsen Honeydew, Ph.D.

Dr. Bunsen Honeydew conducted his first experiment when he was just eight years old—and his hair never grew back. He received his Ph.D. from M.I.T. (the Muppet Institute of Technology), and was appointed chief scientist and social director of Muppet Labs when no one else applied for the job.

WELCOME TO MUPPET LABS, WHERE TOMORROW IS BEING MADE TODAY.

Bright Spark

Before Beaker joined him, Dr. Honeydew tested his own inventions. After a mishap with his patented Muppet Labs Exploding Clothes™, Bunsen hired an assistant.

Without his eyeglasses he is often mistaken for a melon.

Head is not perfectly round, but he hopes to get there some day.

Always wears lab coat when experimenting, or eating a particularly messy lunch.

Secret Recipe

Dr. Honeydew lives his life in search of greater scientific knowledge and the recipe for the perfect grilled cheese sandwich. Only Beaker's dairy allergy stands in the way of Bunsen achieving this.

MUPPET FILE

Debut *The Muppet Show* #108

Favorite Invention
Edible paperclips

Greatest Theoretical Discovery
Silly string theory

37

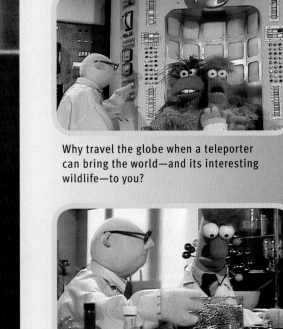

Why travel the globe when a teleporter can bring the world—and its interesting wildlife—to you?

Muppet Labs' amazing edible paper clips are an excellent way of adding extra iron into your diet.

Need more space in your closet? Muppet Labs shrinking pills will make your clothes—and you—smaller.

Cactus Quartet

Hailing from the American west with a song in their hearts and pointy needles everywhere else, the Cactus Quartet performs in close harmony. They never sing flat, but they are occasionally sharp.

DO YOU LIKE THE FOUR-PART HARMONY?

I'D PREFER THEY PLAY SOLO. SO LOW I CAN'T HEAR THEM!

Desert Queen
Quartet fans (both of them) can see the group in a Muppets version of the "Bohemian Rhapsody" music video alongside bananas, flowers, bunnies, and prairie dogs.

Keep It Under Your Hat
Although they are known for singing in a barbershop quartet, none of the cacti are qualified to cut hair. The boys enjoy touring for the moment, but hope someday to put down roots.

Custom-made straw hats

HELLO, HELLO!

HELLOOO!

MUPPET FILE
Debut *Muppets Tonight* #105
Favorite Song "How Dry I Am"
First Album Songs in the Key of Ouch

Camilla

Dreaming of a life in show business from the time she was an egg, Camilla flew the coop, met Gonzo, and hatched a career as the biggest and most plucky performer of her generation. She acts, she dances, she clucks—she's a triple threat.

Only uses cosmetics not tested on animals.

First Date
Camilla and Gonzo's first date was a disaster. His thoughtful gift of flowers triggered Camilla's hay fever and it took weeks for her to stop sneezing.

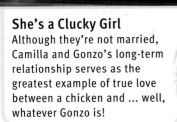

She's a Clucky Girl
Although they're not married, Camilla and Gonzo's long-term relationship serves as the greatest example of true love between a chicken and ... well, whatever Gonzo is!

Big Dreams
Camilla still finds herself typecast in poultry roles, but hopes some day to play her dream part: Blanche DuBois in the play *A Streetcar Named Desire* opposite Gonzo.

BAWK-BYAWK BAWK-BA-CAWWWW

Camilla thinks her wings are her best feature.

Moisturizes daily to keep her wattles supple.

MUPPET FILE
Debut
The Muppet Show #318
Special Talents Crossing the road
Dislikes Rotisseries and barbecues

Chickens

When Kermit saw the talent of this troupe of happy hens while visiting a farm, he hired them on the spot. It didn't hurt that they were prepared to work for chicken feed. Kermit knows to treat the chickens well, however—they are quite a force when together.

WHAT ARE THESE CHICKENS DOING HERE?

SAME THING THE BEAR DOES ON STAGE—LAYING EGGS.

Unique Interpretations
Whether singing Baby Face or Pick a Little, Talk a Little, the chickens know how to sell a song as no one else can.

Feathered Friends
The chickens love hanging out together most of all, but they have forged an awkward friendship with the Swedish Chef. While chefs and chickens are usually enemies, these birds have never ended up in a poultry stew.

Even though they look similar, the chickens are not all related.

BAWK, BAWK, BAWK, BA-CAWK!"

The chickens never leave home without their lashes perfectly groomed.

MUPPET FILE
Debut *The Muppet Musicians of Bremen*
Special Talents Egg laying
Favorite Song "Ain't Nobody Here But Us Chickens"

Clifford

Colorful, catfish-like Clifford has been a musician, a host, and an actor. The multi-colored performer is also multi-talented, playing many musical instruments. His trademark dreadlocks are often paired with a jazzy Hawaiian shirt.

MUPPET FILE

Debut *MuppeTelevision* #1

Favorite Clothing Vests

Special talent Making vests look good

Outfit so colorful, he has to put his shades on to look in the mirror.

Host with the Most
Kermit saw something special behind Clifford's trademark shades and named the magenta man as his first choice to be host of K-MUP's *Muppets Tonight*.

It took years to get his dreads just the way he likes them.

Team Player
Clifford started out in Solid Foam, the *MuppeTelevision* house band alongside Digit, Beard, Flash, and Animal. After his stint as host of *Muppets Tonight*, Clifford put his shades back on for good and happily slipped back into the Muppet ensemble.

Custom tailored clothes by Polly of Passaichere.

Clodhoppers

The **Clodhoppers were** discovered when they accidentally attended an open audition for Muppet dancers while trying to find an audition for the Royal Academy of Arts. They never made it to the Academy.

NOW THAT'S WHAT I CALL A HIP ACT.

AND WE'RE WHAT I CALL A HIP REPLACEMENT.

Multi-talented Muppets
Although mostly known as dancers, the Clodhoppers have also been known to pick up an instrument and play.

Back to the Start
Formally known as The Klunks, the Clodhoppers did the splits when they performed the song "Opposites Attract." They were also once part of a Dixieland band.

Clodhoppers always dance in perfect, ungainly, unison.

MUPPET FILE
Debut *Julie: My Favorite Things* TV special

Special Talents Stomping on bugs

Pet Peeve When people call them clods

They dance in boots because they're the only shoes they could find that fit.

Clueless Morgan

Clueless Morgan received his nickname when he landed his breakthrough role as a pirate in *Muppet Treasure Island* and everyone thought him very naive. His real name isn't much better— Dimwit C. Morgan (the "C" stands for Chucklehead).

MUPPET FILE

Debut
Muppet Treasure Island

Special Talents Sleeping

Education No, thanks

First Mates
Clueless stayed in touch with his *Muppet Treasure Island* co-star Polly Lobster, but the friendship soured when Clueless thought Polly was becoming a selfish shellfish.

Clueless Club
Clueless enjoys breathing and doing his involuntary reflexes. He's a member of DENSA, a club for those with sub-zero IQs.

Clueless thought he had to take music lessons because he has horns.

Earring came in a set of 12 (he purchased curtain rings by mistake).

HUH?

45

Constantine

As a tadpole, Constantine was abandoned by his mother and adopted by the owner of Russia's largest bomb factory. He became a criminal mastermind and expert in explosives, blowing up the scenes of his crimes to cover his little froggy footprints.

Black Belt, Green Frog
A trained martial artist, Constantine can break thick wood planks with a single chop, making him a dreaded enemy of trees everywhere.

A Perfect Match
Constantine has fought hardened criminals and fierce law enforcement agents, but he has never come up against anyone like Miss Piggy.

1 MUPPET FILE

Debut
Muppets Most Wanted

Likes Crime

Dislikes
Punishment.

Special Talents
Thwarting law enforcement, knitting

Distinctive mole on upper lip

Keen eyes will notice short points on Constantine's collar.

IT'S NOT EASY BEING MEAN.

Master of Escape
Even a well-guarded Russian Gulag can't hold Constantine. (If it could, *Muppets Most Wanted* would be a very short movie.)

GESUCHT!
EVILEN FROGGEN

1000,– BELOHNUNG!

SACHE01188829932
**TEILENDER
BERLINER POLIZEI**
INFORMATIONSABTEILUNG

SEX: MÄNNLICH
ALTER: UNBEKANNT

CHARAKTERISTIK
RASSE: FROSCH
HÖHE: 55CM–70CM

GEWICHT: 20KG–25KG
HAAR: GRÜN

BLICK: SCHWARZ
TEINT: GRÜN

Flippered and Dangerous
The "Most Wanted" in the title *Muppets Most Wanted* refers to Constantine, the world's most dangerous frog. He even has a wanted poster (trust us, we can read German). If you see him, stay clear and call the amphibian authorities.

Holiday Time!

Whether they are celebrating a classic reunion in *A Muppet Family Christmas* or adding their own special twist to Charles Dickens in *The Muppet Christmas Carol*, the many Muppet Christmas classics never fail to resonate with viewers. That's because holidays are all about family, and, as weird as they may be, the Muppets are family— not just to each other but to us.

Snowman
Fozzie Bear usually works as a solo performer, but in *A Muppet Family Christmas* he teamed up with a funny snowman. The act broke up after it got a bit warm in the farmhouse.

Turkey
This fast-talking gobbler was invited to (be) dinner in *A Muppet Family Christmas*, but got a last-minute reprieve from the Swedish Chef.

Christmas Present

Miser Ebenezer Scrooge was visited by three ghosts in *The Muppet Christmas Carol*. The Ghost of Christmas Present was a jolly redhead.

Christmas Past

Scrooge was shown a glimpse of himself as a young man thanks to this ethereal floating spirit.

Christmas Yet to Come

This mysterious, hooded, faceless figure gave Scrooge a peek at his bleak future.

Kermit used to joke that if a frog and a pig had children, they would be bouncing baby figs. But, in *The Muppet Christmas Carol*, the happy couple, playing Bob and Emily Cratchit, had two pigs and two frogs. Miss Piggy showed her maternal side.

Tiny Tim
Kermit's nephew Robin played Tiny Tim. Robin got the job because of his truly unique qualifications: he was the only frog who fit the tiny costume.

All in the Family
Before production, Kermit and Piggy spent a weekend with their fictional kids. Piggy is still having nightmare flashbacks of a certain family restaurant food fight.

Roles Filled
After a worldwide search for little frogs and pigs, the role of the pig daughters went to Betina and Belinda Pig, while young Peter the Frog won the role of Peter Cratchit.

Belinda (or is this Betina?)

Betina (or is this Belinda?)

Peter—the little frog NOT on a crutch

Tiny Tim played by tiny frog

GOD BLESS US... EVERY ONE!

MUPPET FILE
Debut *The Muppet Christmas Carol*
Training Miss Piggy's School for Young Performers
Goals To grow taller

Crazy Harry

Crazy Harry is a walking, talking special effect using high explosives to create low humor. Rarely is he involved in anything that doesn't end in major disaster. (Actually, the same could be said for Fozzie Bear, but at least the Bear doesn't cause structural damage.)

Harry's Da Bomb
Harry is always careful to obtain the necessary permits for his explosions. And then he blows them up!

Detonator was a sixth birthday present from his mom.

Crazy Donald
The mean kids on the playground came up with his first nickname, Crazy Donald. But, the cruel name offended the sensitive guy, so he changed it to Crazy Harry instead.

Master Blaster
Harry received his training at the Buchholz School of Pyrotechnics and Cheese-making. He graduated with a major in explosions and a minor in brie.

CRAZY HARRY PLAYS WITH ELECTRICITY!

Brushes twice daily, but never flosses. He lives dangerously.

MUPPET FILE
Debut
The Muppets Valentine Show pilot
Likes Fireworks, firecrackers, and dynamite
Dislikes
Quiet walks on the beach

51

Doglion

He's not a dog, and he's not a lion. He's a ... well, we don't know exactly what he is. But, whatever he is, he's a huge beast of few words and much fur. When not performing, Doglion enjoys looking at, expanding, and curating his thimble collection.

Pampered
After bathing, it takes Doglion two hours (and a team of 14 volunteers) to blow-dry his fur.

LIVA... CRATCH... SCRAN... FLOR!

Angry Feet
Surprisingly, Doglion spent several years studying dance, including modern, jazz, and tap, at the Murray Arthur School of Dance. He broke several school dance records, as well as the feet of 55 instructors.

Visited a waxing salon once. The attendant ran away!

Oh Buoy!
Doglion enjoys spending his spare time on his boat. The watercraft is safety-rated for up to eight passengers, or one incredibly large furry beast.

MUPPET FILE
Debut The Muppet Show #209

Teeth Two

Favorite Book Little Women

Dr. Julius Strangepork

When playing the science officer of the spaceship *Swinetrek*, Julius Strangepork is often puzzled, occasionally befuddled, and almost always clueless—in real life, he's even more so. That's how he got the part. Well, that and he fit the costume.

WHAT DO YOU THINK OF STRANGEPORK?

IT'S NOT ON MY DIET.

German of the Board

Hailing from a small town near Hamelburg, Julius Strangepork studied science, acting and speaking with a weird accent at Berlin Polytechnic.

Enjoys listening to hog calls and polkas.

IS THIS THING ON?

Spacesuit can withstand vacuum of space, but is not machine washable.

MUPPET FILE

Debut *The Muppet Show #203*

Likes Playing with robots

Dislikes Pigs who hog the swill stroganoff ... namely, Link Hogthrob

Dr. Phil Van Neuter

THIS GUY IS A WEIRDO.

NO WONDER HE FITS IN WITH THE MUPPETS.

Phil Van Neuter studied taxidermy at Stufts University, then attended the Ho-Ho-Kus, New Jersey School of Veterinary Medicine, majoring in Mad Science with a minor in Cake Decorating. He has a primary interest in weird phenomena and a passion for theater.

For a school exam, Phil performed brain surgery on himself.

To save money, Phil's assistant trims his sideburns. His ears have been sewn back on twice.

Dr. Love

Dr. Van Neuter left his single life behind when he married his assistant's sister, the enchanting Composta Heap. Someday, they hope to raise a family of test tube babies.

SCARED YOU, DIDN'T I?

Dr. Phil's rubber gloves are far more dirty than anything he is likely to touch.

MUPPET FILE

Debut *Muppets Tonight* #104

Special Talents Surgery

Pet Peeves When people are peeved at their pets

Tales of the Unnatural

Dr. Phil hosted *Tales from the Vet*, an anthology of animal horror stories like "The Turkey Who Loved Thanksgiving" and "Percy the Ham-eating Pig."

Dr. Teeth

Founder, keyboardist, and spiritual leader of The Electric Mayhem band, Dr. Teeth is the king of cool, the master of mellow, and all-around laid-back legendary music master. He famously has a dazzling, wide smile and a gold tooth.

To the Rescue
Dr. Teeth saved the day in *The Muppet Movie*, when his reading of the heavy duty script led to the discovery of our stranded heroes.

Chairman of the Keyboard
Dr. Teeth sometimes takes a solo behind the keyboard. His voice has been compared to singer Dr. John, a comparison that flatters the Muppet music master.

The Doctor is Way Out
Music experts consider Dr. Teeth to be one of the best keyboard players in the history of music. Dr. Teeth makes any song come alive with his psychedelic musicianship.

Visits to his dental hygienist sometimes take days.

GOLDEN TEETH AND TONES... WELCOME TO MY PRESENCE!

Natural hair color— burnt orange.

His fingers are insured.

MUPPET FILE
Debut
The Muppet Show pilot
Likes Getting down
Dislikes
Visiting the dental hygenist

ELECTRIC MAYHEM

The Electric Mayhem is the house band on *The Muppet Show*. They first played as a group in 1975. While they are usually associated with the Muppets, die-hard fans will remember their early live tours, opening for the little known band, Die-Hard.

Janice: All natural products keep her hair shiny.

Dr. Teeth: Most valuable mouth in the band.

CAN YOU DIG IT?

DRUMS! DRUMS!

Animal: Wide mouth makes it easy to breathe when he's drumming hard.

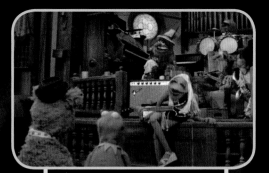

Big Break
Kermit's disovery of the band was dramatized in *The Muppet Movie*. In real life, however, Kermit didn't find the band in a church, but at an all-night dry cleaners, where Animal was being steamed and pressed.

Floyd Pepper: Secretly owns a Barry Manilow record.

HUH?

Zoot: His trademark fedora is being cleaned.

GROOVE IT, BABY!

Gone Bananas

Fozzie's Ma has always supported her son's interest in comedy. For one birthday, she gave him this limited edition banana and Gags Beasley's not-so-best-selling book, *1001 Banana Jokes*.

MA! I CAN'T HEAR YOU! I GOT A BANANA IN MY EAR!

(That's joke #127.)

Emily Bear

NICE LADY.

FUNNIER THAN HER SON.

Emily Bear (a.k.a. Ma Bear) is Fozzie's beloved mother. She is a proud supporter of her son's career, even if she doesn't quite care for his freaky friends. Since her darling cub has gone out into the world, she enjoys traveling and taking surfing lessons.

Emily went prematurely gray soon after Fozzie's birth.

The Family Fozzie
Neither Fozzie nor his mother mention Fozzie's dad. He is most likely hibernating or has landed a job as a rug in a hunting lodge.

I LOVE MY SON, BUT I'M NOT TOO SURE ABOUT HIS WEIRDO FRIENDS.

Just Right
Emily Bear's farmhouse is an inviting place. She keeps bees for the honey, cows for the milk, and raises chickens for the eggs (and to have someone to play cards with).

Emily makes her own lace in her spare time.

MUPPET FILE
Debut The Muppet Show #216

Species Ursus Mommius

Favorite Non-bear Comedian Buddy Hackett

Fazoobs

Planet Koozebane is home to many species, the most musical of which are the Fazoobs. The Fazoobs are their own instruments, which is handy but gives their roadies very little to do during concert tours. While they are almost unknown on Earth, they are even more unknown on Koozebane!

DO YOU BELIEVE IN INTELLIGENT LIFE ON OTHER PLANETS?

WELL, THERE CERTAINLY ISN'T ANY ON THIS ONE!

Oh, The Pain!
The Fazoobs' audition for *The Muppet Show* did not go well, but immediately afterward, the group booked a TV gig— playing a headache in a painkiller commercial.

Alien Nation
In an effort to blend in, the Fazoobs once tried wearing matching T-shirts reading "We Are Not Aliens From Another Planet," but realized they attracted even more attention!

Thinks he's the leader

Spends 10 minutes each day tuning his snout

Is literally a drumhead

MUPPET FILE
Debut
The Muppet Show #208
Likes The Milky Way
Dislikes
All other candy bars

Fleet Scribbler

Gossip writer for *The Daily Scandal*, Fleet Scribbler is known for his aggressive pursuit of the facts, and his complete lack of interest in reporting them. Shameless Fleet creates the most sensational headline he can think of first, and then finds a story to back it up.

Digging for Dirt

When his subjects were unwilling to talk, sneaky Scribbler went through their garbage. He learned a lot of their dirty little secrets and had to launder a lot of his dirty little clothing.

Piece of cheese somewhere in hair from the last time an angry celebrity threw a plate at him.

Good Riddance

Fleet eventually grew tired of being disliked by everyone he met. He traded in his notebook and camera for a job that would make him even less popular —a tax auditor.

Sunglasses hide Fleet's face and emotions from people.

Language Skills

To help him sniff out stories, Fleet learned several languages. He even studied mock Swedish— though there's only one other person we know of who speaks it—the Swedish Chef.

Controversial buttons to provoke reactions

MUPPET FILE

Debut
The Muppet Show #204

Occupation
Tabloid Journalist

Training
Little Buckaroo School of Rodeo and Journalism

Arm broken three times by angry interviewees

Fletcher Bird

Fletcher Bird is a rare bird with a rare talent for dance. He developed his passion while still in the egg—his nest was located above a ballet theater. Fletcher got a scholarship in dance (to fill the birds quota), but once in school, he excelled on his own merits.

Visits a plumage stylist every week.

First Class Flyer
Unlike the ostrich and other large birds, Fletcher can fly. In fact, he holds membership cards in several airline frequent flier clubs.

Winging It
Although trained in ballet, Fletcher also loves modern dance, jazz dance, and an occasional Charleston. Tap is a bit of a problem—he has trouble finding tap shoes that fit giant birds.

Nobody knows what Fletcher's natural feather color is.

MUPPET FILE
Debut
The Muppet Show #302

Education Royal Avian Dance Academy of Covent Garden

Special talent
Molting

Stripy tights keep his legs warm and supple for all the dancing.

Floyd Pepper

Floyd Pepper is the bass player for The Electric Mayhem rock band. Although his first love is jazz, Floyd joined the Mayhem because it paid better. It turned out to be a more challenging job than he thought. As well as keeping the rhythm, he had to keep Animal on his chain and out of trouble.

Seriously Groovy
Floyd takes his grooviness very seriously. He once threatened to leave *The Muppet Show* for artistic reasons—he hated the theme song.

> I AM THE HIPPEST OF THE HIP.

In Harmony
Floyd hesitates to put a label on his relationship with Janice, but he will admit they have lots of musical fun together.

Floyd calls his bass "Ethel."

MUPPET FILE
Debut
The Muppet Show pilot
Likes Cool Jazz, Rock 'n' Roll, Janice
Dislikes
Easy listening

Dinner With Kermit

Eating with the Muppets is always an extreme experience—and in *Muppets Most Wanted*, a fancy meal in a swanky Hollywood eatery opens the door to international adventure and intrigue.

The Flying Zucchini Brothers

Booma-booma!

Marco, Giuseppi, Luigi, Lorenzo, Heathcliff, and their siblings come from a long line of performing Zucchinis. Even as children, they proved defying gravity was in their blood when they used the playground see-saws to catapult each other into the air.

The Only Way to Fly
The Zucchini Brothers fly in the footsteps of their idols, the Zacchini Brothers, inventors of the human cannonball act.

Of the Highest Caliber
The Brothers made a huge impact on show business with their five-cannon launch. They also made a huge impact on the stage.

EGGPLANT PARMIGIANA!

Bad case of helmet hair

What's In a Name?
The Zucchini family was once named "Squash," but changed it because it seemed a bad name for a human cannonball act.

MANNICOTTI!

RAVIOLI!

Flying Zucchini symbol from family coat of arms

Custom-made cannon ensures a snug fit.

MUPPET FILE
Debut
The Muppet Show #208
Special talent Going ballistic
Favorite Song
"Fly Me To The Moon"

Foo-Foo

Miss Piggy knows that you can't be a true superstar without the ultimate diva accessory: an adorable little dog. Foo-Foo is Miss Piggy's beloved pet, and as far as Miss Piggy is concerned, she can do no wrong—as long as she doesn't take too much attention away from Piggy herself.

Poodle Posse
Foo-Foo is a pedigree toy poodle with several distinguished siblings: Oui-Oui, Poo-Poo, Num-Num, Goo-Goo, and Fred.

Dog Vs. Frog
Who doesn't like Kermit? Well, it seems that Foo-Foo is one of the few creatures on the planet who is not a fan of the world's most famous frog. Maybe she's jealous of Kermit's place in Piggy's heart.

Big Break
Foo-Foo once got a chance to become a performing dog act on *The Muppet Show*. She showed that, like her owner, she doesn't like to follow commands.

Ears perk up on hearing Miss Piggy's voice (as long as she's not singing).

Diamond collar by Hairy Winston, dog Jeweler

MUPPET FILE

Debut The Muppet Show #404
Likes The finer things
Dislikes Frogs

Grooming by Madame Rollin of Ronkonkoma

BOW WOW!

Strange on a Train
In *Muppets Most Wanted*, the gang tours Europe aboard a ramshackle railroad car. Fozzie enjoyed it even more than sitting at home going "chugga-chugga-wooo-wooo!"

Fozzie Bear

Fozzie's jokes might be terrible, but everyone loves him because he never stops trying. As Kermit says, "He's a very trying bear." As a cub, Fozzie became hooked on comedy when his family hibernated in the Catskill Mountains and he stayed through the summer to watch top comics work in the resorts there.

Sensitive Soul
Fozzie is a naturally sensitive bear, but over the years Statler and Waldorf's insults have helped him develop a thick skin (which is covered up by soft and cuddly fur).

Dummy Up
A brief venture into ventriloquism went nowhere due to Fozzie's inability to speak without moving his lips—largely because he doesn't actually have lips.

Bear Meets Frog
While not officially a team, Fozzie and Kermit have worked together often and enjoy a natural sense of comic timing.

Fozzie has many identical hats. He thinks this one is the funniest.

You can tell Fozzie from other bears by his lack of teeth.

WOCKA-WOCKA!

MUPPET FILE
Debut
The Muppet Show #101

Likes Making people laugh

Dislikes Hibernation and hecklers

Fozzie only buys his accessories from shops with names that are "funn-ee!"

Frackles

Frackles are a unique species of Muppet monster, though most have a pointy beak or snout. If you see a sharp-beaked creature covered by fur and feathers, you're either seeing a Frackle or having a particularly weird nightmare.

DO YOU THINK FRACKLES HAVE FRECKLES?

I'M NOT GETTING CLOSE ENOUGH TO FIND OUT.

Last Dance
Frackles are mean and stubborn, but strangely graceful on the dance floor—if you overlook their habit of eating their partners.

Bolshy blue Frackle

Jade green hunchbacked Frackle

Monster Mix-up
All Frackles are monsters, but not all monsters are Frackles. This distinction is really only of concern to Frackles, monsters, and a few die-hard Muppets fans.

Grumpy green Frackle

THE TIMES
ernment tries to neutralize
aker's ruling on Bill

Angry G.
Sir Har
list conf

Offer to change

MUPPET FILE
Debut *The Great Santa Claus Switch*
Likes Children (when properly seasoned)
Dislikes Foods that are low in fiber

Fozzie's Best Jokes

Fozzie Bear, the Muppets' own stand-up comedian, uses only the best comedy material sent to him by Gags Beasley, the legendary writer of the banana sketch. Unfortunately, Gags sends his best material to his other clients.

HEY! QUESTION: WHAT HAS A THOUSAND LEGS, BUT CAN'T WALK? 500 PAIRS OF PANTS!

I KNOW A GUY WHO'S SO CHEAP— WHEN HE GOES FISHING HE PUTS A PICTURE OF A WORM ON HIS HOOK AND HE CATCHES A PICTURE OF A FISH.

MY COUSIN IS SO THIN HE PAINTS HIS HEAD GOLD AND RENTS HIMSELF OUT AS A FLAGPOLE.
ONE CANNIBAL SAYS TO THE OTHER CANNIBAL: "WHO WAS THAT LADY I SAW YOU WITH LAST NIGHT?" THE OTHER CANNIBAL SAYS "THAT WAS NO LADY, THAT WAS MY LUNCH!"
WHAT DO YOU GET WHEN YOU CROSS AN ESKIMO AND A PIG? A POLAR BOAR!

Frog Scouts

Young frogs looking for fun, friendship, and a spirited game of leapfrog can find it in the Frog Scouts. Kermit's nephew Robin belongs to Okefenokee Pack 12. They may like camping and marching, but their true passion is rock music.

> WERE YOU EVER A SCOUT?

> YUP. I GOT A MERIT BADGE IN HECKLING WILDLIFE.

Leader of the Pack
Frog Scout Pack 12 is under the leadership and supervision of Miss Applebee, who is also a professional leapfrog coach.

High-achieving Frogs
The Scouts are always pursuing new merit badges. Pack 12 frogs have earned merit badges in Air Conditioning Repair and Nuclear Fission.

> DO WE GET A MERIT BADGE FOR BEING IN THIS BOOK?

Working on his Cat's Cradle merit badge, but doesn't have a cat.

Cap purchased from The Little Frog Store

Toy binoculars for looking at toys from far distances

MUPPET FILE
Debut *The Muppet Show* #509

Likes Hiking and fly fishing (for flies, not fish)

Dislikes Trite romantic comedies

George the Janitor

Of all the unsung backstage heroes of the Muppets, George the Janitor is probably the most unsung-est, working to keep the backstage area clean. A surly, grumpy guy, only one thing seems to make George happy—his mop.

I HAVEN'T SEEN GEORGE IN A WHILE.

ME NEITHER. HE FINALLY WISED UP AND GOT OUT OF HERE.

Swept off his Feet

Although he prefers to spend time with his mop, George has occasionally joined Mildred out on the dance floor. The mop doesn't get jealous anymore.

Once took his mop on a date and insisted they split the check.

From Tired to Retired

George retired quite some time ago, passing on his duties to Beauregard. Sometimes, he unexpectedly returns to sweep—he has a serious case of sweepwalking.

Uses actual elbow grease on his elbow when cleaning.

MUPPET FILE

Debut The Muppets Valentine Show pilot

Favorite Pastime Organizing the broom closet

Dislikes Waxy yellow buildup

75

Geri and the Atrics

Born to be Wild
To celebrate the release of their album, *Staying Alive— Barely*, the band embarked on a tour of assisted living facilities of the American southwest.

Cello player Geri formed her band, the Atrics, while living in the Happy Heart Rest Home. Now Geri and her band live on a tour bus stocked with an endless supply of prune juice, iron supplements, and hard candies. Those ladies know how to rock (in chairs).

WELL, HELLO THERE!

WHAT ARE YOU DOING AFTER THE SHOW, LADIES?

Age Against the Machine
Geri and the Atrics and Bobby Benson's Baby Band once did a world tour. Venues lost big when they didn't stock enough soft foods and diapers for the crowd.

Her shades are cool—and hide her wrinkly eyes.

Formerly played in the group the Hot Flashes.

Wishes her grandchildren would call more often.

Her pacemaker helps keep the beat.

MUPPET FILE
Debut The Muppet Show #101

First Album *Meet the Atrics*

Special Talents Falling asleep anywhere, any time

Gladys the Cafeteria Lady

What's cooking?

When the Swedish Chef opened a canteen at the Muppet Theater for the cast and crew, Gladys came on board to wait tables. She took on this job after years of cleaning greasy spoons at a variety of greasy spoons.

Once considered using contact lenses, but couldn't locate her eyes.

Cake Topper
The Muppet canteen also catered special events. But, with the Swedish Chef in charge of cooking, the events became somewhat less special.

No Glad in Gladys
Surly, grumpy, and unpleasant, Gladys had no problem putting people in their place. Unfortunately for business, that place was usually far away from the canteen.

Used to be called Sally, but changed her name after she found a good deal on a necklace.

Once swapped flowers with Fozzie and squirted everyone.

Cantina Banned
Despite Gladys's best efforts, the Muppet Theater canteen closed for good after one too many cases of food poisoning.

MUPPET FILE
Debut *The Muppet Show #301*
Likes Big tippers
Dislikes People who don't eat all their food

Gonzo the Great!
Daredevil Gonzo once attempted "head bowling." It all went wrong when Dr. Bunsen Honeydew realized that the remote controlled ball he invented had come to life.

GONZO (a.k.a. The Great Gonzo)

Whether engaging in his unique performance art, singing a song, taking on a serious acting role, or fixing the plumbing, The Great Gonzo is willing to try anything once. And he'll gladly do it again if it's particularly painful.

Say Cheese!
In The *Great Muppet Caper*, photographer Gonzo took a picture of the audience and promised to send each of them a copy. Did you receive yours?

Author! Author!
Gonzo left his crash helmet behind and stretched his acting talent to play Charles Dickens in *The Muppet Christmas Carol*. Old photos of the actual author show little resemblance to Gonzo— Dickens' nose was smaller.

The Great Gonzo
His vague origins instilled in Gonzo a strong desire to find a place where he belongs. This search led him to the Muppets. Gonzo once left the Muppets to become a movie star in India, but soon returned when he realized he had forgotten his toothbrush.

Exercises his nose muscles regularly— he can curl up his schnoz on command.

Shops for clothes at "Slattery's Small and Geeky."

MUPPET FILE
Debut *The Great Santa Claus Switch*

Likes Pushing his creative boundaries to new and painful levels

Dislikes High insurance rates

Picture Imperfect
Even an ordinary portrait session becomes a daredevil stunt when The Great Gonzo is involved. Shortly after this photo was taken, Gonzo dove from his stool into a tiny bucket of oatmeal. The photographer is still cleaning up.

Gonzo's Great Acts

Never before in the history of show business has there been a performer quite like The Great Gonzo. (And, if he keeps trying these daring stunts, there won't be one for much longer!)

Geek on Wire

Gonzo's stunts are not just about irrational risk. He is an artist whose art is a tightrope walk between culture and danger. He demonstrates that concept with the help of some friends in his wire walk. (It was their idea to use the net.)

Gonzo's boots have hard steel toes, but soft cushy insoles.

Steely-eyed look of concentration (or indigestion)

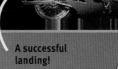

A successful landing!

OH, GIVE ME A HOME, WHERE THE BUFFALO ROAM...

Born to be Wild

One of Gonzo's more conventional acts of "lunatic daring" was jumping a motorcycle into Statler and Waldorf's box. His original plan was to jump from the theater's roof into Waldorf's car, a 1939 Dodge coupe, but he couldn't get the proper permits.

Capes have a tendency to get snagged and stuck, creating dangerous situations. This is exactly why he wears one.

Horsing Around

To appeal to his cowboy fans, Gonzo developed a western-themed act in which he stood on stilts connected to a horse's stirrups and rode at full gallop while singing "Home on the Range." His only performance was cut short by a low bridge.

Dressed to Thrill

Gonzo's uniform is waterproof, fireproof, and shock-resistant. It was built to protect him from most things except his own foolishness. The designers were unable to test it completely. After all, who knows what Gonzo will do next?

Tail extension: The horse lost much of his tail hair from the stress of rehearsing this stunt.

YOU'RE OFF-KEY... AND MY STIRRUPS HURT!

Gorgon Heap

Gorgon Heap is a graduate of a top ivy-league university where he gained a taste for ivy and the finer things (and people). A world-class eater, Gorgon has spent a lifetime tracking down the best chefs... and eating them.

Which Words to Chews?
Gorgon considers himself to be the strong silent type. After all, actions speak louder than words. And it's rude to speak with your mouth full.

By a Nose
Gorgon wore a fake nose when he and Lenny the Lizard re-enacted the classic Muppet performance, "Glow Worm". Lenny avoided being eaten by holding on to Gorgon's tonsils.

You May Eat a Stranger
A music lover, Gorgon put an early end to Wayne and Wanda's performance of "Some Enchanted Evening."

Uses eye drops to keep his eyes yellow.

In high school, Gorgon was voted most likely to inhale New Jersey.

MUPPET FILE
Debut
The Muppet Show pilot

Likes Haute cuisine

Dislikes Cold cuisine

DELICIOUS!

Hilda

An unsung hero of the Muppets, Hilda is the seamstress responsible for avoiding wardrobe malfunctions. She is a sweet lady with a unique European accent and a talent for keeping her actors in stitches.

Young at Heart
Although her friends regard her as ageless, Hilda once tried a full makeover to appear younger. The makeover was underwhelming.

Sew Creative
Hilda has retired from show business and now makes hand-made tea cozies for people whose teapots don't feel cozy enough.

Busy Backstage
Hilda sometimes appeared in sketches, but she was usually busy with costumes—except when preparing Kermit's costume. His collar requires limited maintenance.

Hilda tried trading in her round glasses, but these didn't go with her head.

Once sat on her pin cushion, leaving her with pins and needles.

MUPPET FILE
Debut *The Muppet Show* #102
Special Talents Stitching in time, saving nine
Favorite Sewing-related Word Bobbin

85

Hobos

In *The Muppets*, a scruffy trio of Hobos wandered into the Muppet Theater looking for a place to warm up. They were treated to a great view of the Muppet Telethon and violated fire department regulations with a toasty-warm bonfire.

I CAN'T BELIEVE THOSE HOBOS WANDERED INTO THE MUPPET THEATER.

ISN'T THEIR LIFE HARD ENOUGH?

Bargain Bindle
Like all hobos they carry their stuff in a bindle—a bandana tied to a stick. But since these are Hollywood hobos, they only use designer bindles.

Hobo Code
Unlike tramps or bums, hobos are willing to work. These Hobos received Ph.D.s in Hobo Arts from Vagabond University, located on Freight Car #6 on the Baltimore & Ohio.

Fourth-generation hobo on his mother's side

Has not removed his coat in four weeks.

MUPPET FILE
Debut *The Muppets*
Likes Hopping freight trains, eating mulligan stew
Dislikes Being mistaken for bums

Howard Tubman

Originally appearing as an extra, Howard Tubman impressed Kermit with his acting ability. Tubman prepared to portray a wealthy boar by taking all the play money out of his board games and trying to spend it.

Treading the Boars
Howard's first love is musical theater choreography, though no stages can currently support his weight.

Weight and See
Howard is usually sensitive, occasionally frantic, and always hungry. Despite his big appetite, he was teased for years for being the smallest in his family.

The Pig Time
The Tubmans of Porksmith featured Howard as a pig living high on the hog. His long-suffering butler Carter helps him accomplish challenging tasks like getting unstuck from chairs.

Once tried to store some extra snacks inside his cheeks, but kept eating them.

Colonial Rum Cake is his favorite, but anything will do in a pinch.

MUPPET FILE
Debut
Muppets Tonight #105
Likes All cakes except rice cakes
Dislikes
Buffets with time limits

Jacques Roach

Cockroaches are notoriously hard to get rid of, and Jacques is no exception—he has reinvented himself many times. He first appeared on Muppet Television as a Jacques Cousteau-inspired explorer aboard a ship and later played a feisty French chef.

Pirate Pest
Jacques Roach joined the pirate crew of the *Hispaniola* in *Muppet Treasure Island*.

Roach Coach
Chef Jacques faced off against the Swedish Chef in an unappetizing cooking show. Fortunately for viewers, the short-lived show was not usually broadcast at mealtimes.

Bug Voyage
In his spare time, Jacques Roach uses his seagoing and culinary experience to lead foodie tours of cruise ship galleys for his fellow cockroaches.

Jacques is writing a book about a cockroach who turns into a man.

Difficult to find a roach-sized hat. He bought a turtle hat and had it altered.

MUPPET FILE
Debut *MuppeTelevision* #2

Likes Scuttling under the fridge when the lights come on

Dislikes Children with magnifying glasses

Janice

Hailing from California, Janice is the easygoing lead guitarist for The Electric Mayhem band. After a brief tour in an all-girl group called The Sunflower Seeds, she found her true home with The Electric Mayhem, and a deep emotional link with bass player Floyd Pepper.

Guitar Girl
Janice auditioned for Dr. Teeth with a non-stop 48-minute guitar riff. Dr. Teeth was impressed, so Janice didn't tell him that her performance was just the result of getting her fingers stuck in the strings.

Sick Humor
As one of Dr. Bob's nurses, Janice delivered her share of punch lines in Veterinarian's Hospital.

Keeps hair shiny with mink oil provided by a friendly mink.

Plugged In
Janice is one of the world's greatest left-handed guitar players. She is basically self-taught, though Floyd has given her some private music lessons.

MUPPET FILE

Debut *The Muppet Show* pilot

Likes Sun, sand, and organic smoothies

Dislikes Bad vibes

Muppet Parodies

The Muppets have always poked gentle fun at their fellow pop culture stars, but they're not being mean. It all comes from love, respect, and a desire to create posters and calendars that can cover up hideous wallpaper.

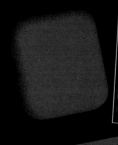

The Dogfather
Rowlf made criminals an offer they couldn't refuse as the famous Dog Don.

Go Figure
As secret agent Jamie Pond 006½, Kermit's biggest adventure was convincing Miss Piggy to be painted gold.

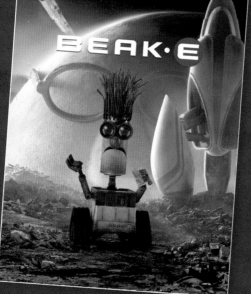

Beak-E
Beaker discovered an upside to being the last one on a desolate planet— he got to be away from the hazards of Muppet Labs.

Hammah Montana
Miss Piggy struggled with this two-sided role. She was great playing someone famous, but not so good at being a normal person.

Piggy Woman
Miss Piggy loved the fact that this movie took place in a fancy hotel suite. When shooting ended, she refused to move out.

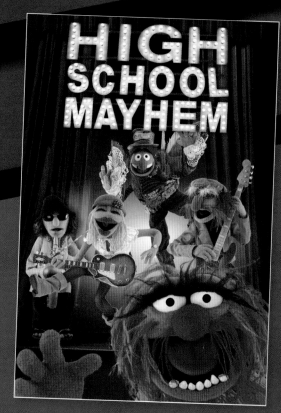

High School Mayhem
The Electric Mayhem went back to high school to put on a big musical—and this time they almost got their diplomas.

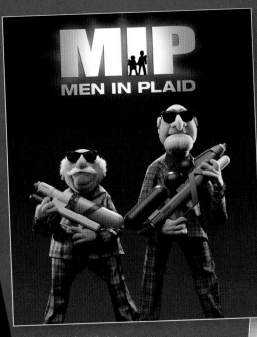

Men in Plaid
Statler and Waldorf kept the world safe from aliens and their lawns safe from neighborhood kids.

ON THE HIGH SEAS, IT'S EASY TURNING GREEN.

PIRATES of the AMPHIBIAN
AT WIT'S END

Pirates of the Amphibian: At Wit's End
Captain Kermit is the most lovable rogue to sail the six seas (he's never been to the seventh, but he's going there on vacation next year).

Javas

DOESN'T IT BOTHER YOU THAT THEIR ACT ALWAYS ENDS THE SAME WAY?

WHO CARES? AS LONG AS IT ENDS.

These mysterious creatures are known for one thing, and one thing only—their performance to the brassy song, "Java." They spontaneously created their dance when they first heard the song. They dance to it every time they hear it—whether you want them to or not.

A Big Finish
Every act needs a big finish, and these guys end their number with a blast—literally. Thanks to the magic of special effects, no Javas are hurt in the making of the show.

Can't wait to hear more trumpet music.

Java Jive
It was once thought that the Javas originated from the exotic island of Java, but they actually come from Brooklyn.

Has had a long day of listening to trumpet music.

Has trouble shopping for shoes.

MUPPET FILE
Debut
Al Hirt's *Fanfare*
Special talents Dancing, explosions
Favorite song
Anything but "Java"

Johnny Fiama

A unique song stylist and proud mama's boy, Johnny Fiama grew up in Camden, New Jersey, where he sang in restaurants. Eventually, he did get booked as a singer, at a "Sons of South Jersey" dance, where he was a big hit.

Vinyl Cut
Johnny's first album was accidentally released without his vocal track. The correct version was released, but the instrumental-only version actually sold better.

Monkey Business
Johnny is rarely seen without his monkey bodyguard and valet, Sal Monella. Johnny met Sal in a grocery store where the monkey was eating ice cream out of the freezer.

Here's Johnny!
Johnny thought his talk show, *The Johnny Fiama Show*, could lead to a new career as a talk show host. It didn't. And it didn't do much for his old career either.

WAIT. IS THAT MY CUE?

Johnny won this ring in an arcade claw machine.

Suit by Gene's Pin-Stripery

MUPPET FILE
Debut *Muppets Tonight* #102
Favorite singer Tony Bennett
Favorite Cologne Mama's sauce

Jowls and the Muppets Tonight Band

A new band was needed for *Muppets Tonight* when The Electric Mayhem were on tour. Jowls (an old friend of Lips), went to audition with his band. Specializing in Zydeco, Jowls' fresh sound passed the audition. They were the only band that showed up.

Zydeco-stars

Wrinkle in Time
Even as a young boy, Jowls had his signature wrinkles and heavy jowls. In second grade, he won a Halloween costume contest by dressing up as a raisin.

Has not removed hat in 12 years.

Wears shades to keep the bags under his eyes from drooping to his feet.

House Guests
Jowls' band became the house band for *Muppets Tonight*. Unfortunately, noise regulations prevent them from playing in any actual houses.

YOW! YOW! OOO, YOU COOL?

Jowls' whistling is heard at the start of every *Muppets Tonight* episode.

When told to turn the other cheek, it takes him hours.

MUPPET FILE
Debut *Muppets Tonight* #101
Likes Cajun food
Dislikes People who like Zydeco just to sound trendy

J.P. Grosse

J.P. Grosse is Scooter's uncle and the greedy owner of the Muppet Theater. He once planned to tear down the theater and put up a junkyard on the property. He abandoned the expensive demolition plans in favor of waiting for the building to fall apart by itself.

J.P. GROSSE GIVES GRUMPY PEOPLE A BAD NAME.

YEAH! WHO DOES HE THINK HE IS... US?

Wild eyebrows keep his forehead warm.

Land Grabber
Ruthless Mr. Grosse gained his vast amount of real estate the old fashioned way—by cheating widows and the rightful owners out of it.

You're Fired!
When J.P. Grosse is angry, he goes around firing anyone he sees. In fact, he has an assistant whose only job is to walk ahead of Grosse and hire people, just so Grosse can fire them moments later.

Has water in his pocket to keep flower fresh.

Charges Kermit rent for use of coffee cup.

MUPPET FILE
Debut
The Muppet Show #205
Likes Cash, checks, wire transfers (accepting, not spending)
Dislikes
Donating to charity

Kermit the Frog

Kermit was born as one of approximately 2,353 tadpoles to Mr. and Mrs. "The Frog" in Leland, Mississippi. He knew at an early age that he wanted to be an entertainer when he performed a soft shoe routine for his relatives (before he even had feet).

A Simple Frog
Although Kermit the Frog has accomplished much in his career and is known and loved by millions of fans, he still considers himself just "your average talking show business frog."

HI-HO, KERMIT THE FROG HERE!

Rainbow Selection
After being discovered by Bernie the Agent, Kermit made the trip to Hollywood and signed his legendary "Standard Rich and Famous" contract. (Maybe he should have read the fine print first.)

Host with the Most
Kermit is best known for being one of the world's leading amphibian entertainers—and for his relationship with a certain pig.

Eleven points on his collar (trust us, we counted the ones on the back that you can't see).

Wiry, but strong. Can bench press three pounds (or one Euro).

MUPPET FILE
Debut
Sam and Friends

Likes Singing, dancing, making people happy

Dislikes
Chaos, pigs seeking a commitment

Koozebanians

Way, way out

Of all the Muppets, the Koozebanians have the longest commute to work. The exact location of the planet Koozebane is unknown, but it is believed to be just down the road from Alpha Centauri, give or take a light year. Its main industry is making more Koozebanians.

Spacey Invaders
The Koozebanian High Council once considered invading Earth, but after watching *The Muppet Show* they cancelled their plans.

Out of this World
Kermit the Frog brought us our first look at Planet Koozebane, and earned himself an enormous amount of frequent flier mileage.

Alien Nation
The main residents of Koozebane share their planet with many other species. The Fazoobs, the Merdlidops, the Spooble, and the Phoob all live in harmony on Koozebane —until they get eaten.

WONK!! WONK!!!

The female of the species. Isn't she lovely?

Male of the species. He is considered tall and handsome on Koozebane.

MUPPET FILE

Debut
The Muppets Valentine Show pilot

Special Talents The Galley-oh Hoop-Hoop courtship ritual

Likes *Star Wars*

Dislikes *Star Peace*

The Romance of Kermit and Miss Piggy

One of the most enduring romances of our time is the love story of Miss Piggy and her magnificent obsession, Kermit the Frog. For decades, the determined diva has relentlessly pursued her beloved frog through thick and thin. And for decades, the frog has kept himself fit by always remaining just a few hops ahead of her.

Table for Two
On their first date (dramatized in *The Muppet Movie*) Kermit treated Miss Piggy to a romantic dinner for two and a very cheap bottle of wine.

Instant Bond
For Miss Piggy, it was love at first sight. During a glee club performance she locked eyes on Kermit—and she hasn't let go since.

Pig O' My Heart
Kermit does have feelings for Piggy, he just wants to keep his personal life private. It's a concept Piggy and her 37 publicists don't understand.

Persistent Piggy
After several fictional weddings, Miss Piggy still lives in hope of the real thing. She carries a marriage license in her purse in case of emergency.

Lenny the Lizard

There are more than 9,000 reptile species and we have no idea to which Lenny belongs—but we do know he is part chameleon. He tried to get a job as Kermit's stand-in, but he lost it when he started changing color during lighting tests.

Internally Grateful
Kermit gave Lenny his big break by casting him in a recreation of Kermit's classic Glow Worm. Lenny was thrilled until he found out the ending involved getting eaten.

Night Crawler
Lenny's somewhat sinister appearance makes him a perfect character for spooky surroundings, but he still sleeps with a nightlight.

HI-HO, LENNY THE LIZARD HERE! YAAAAAAAAY

Host? Or Toast?
During an open audition, Lenny demonstrated his talent as a master of ceremonies. He didn't get the job because Kermit was running the audition and was perfectly happy with the current emcee—himself.

Lack of shoulders makes buying clothes a challenge.

Longer arms than most lizards, also more talkative than most lizards.

MUPPET FILE
Debut *The Muppet Show* #103

Special Talent Regenerating a severed tail

Dislikes Having his tail severed

Leprechauns

Not all leprechauns are fictional. Some of them are not only real but they work as a crack team of security guards in *Muppets Most Wanted*. Unfortunately for the Irish National Bank, the leprechaun guards don't have the same level of luck as their fictional counterparts.

You Wish!

Unlike the leprechauns of myth, Muppet leprechauns can't grant wishes. Not that they would even if they could. In fact, they won't even give you a lift to the airport.

> TO GET OUT OF THIS BOOK.

> IF A LEPRECHAUN GRANTED YOU A WISH, WHAT WOULD IT BE?

Star symbolizes their work in security.

Not a natural redhead, but dyed his hair to fit in.

MUPPET FILE

Debut Muppets Most Wanted

Hometown Dublin, Ireland

Special Talents Guarding gold

103

Lew Zealand

Lew Zealand comes from a long line of boomerang fish throwers. He spent his youth on the New Jersey shore with his rod and reel, where he gave a whole new meaning to "catch and release." With Lew it was more like "release and catch."

Tune-A-Fish
Lew really stretched his creative range with his singing fish act. Sadly, the act didn't go swimmingly and he lost his place in the show.

Playing Koi
With incredible enthusiasm, Lew never flounders and always puts his sole into his work. He has never called in sick—even when he had a painful haddock.

Fish oil keeps his hair pointy.

> *I THROW THEEE FISH AWAY, AND THEY COME BACK TO MEEE!*

Lew's favorite fish, Jerry

MUPPET FILE
Debut *The Muppet Show* #310
Likes Cape Cod
Dislikes Crabby people
Favorite TV Show *Flipper*

Link Hogthrob

Ham actor Link Hogthrob has striking good looks (for a pig), and is always both impeccably groomed and tightly girdled. On the outside, there's no doubt that Link has got it "going on"—which is good, because inside, there's not much going on at all.

Hamming it Up
He is best known for "Pigs in Space" and "Bear on Patrol," but Link hopes to explore his dramatic side soon and play Hamlet. He's just not sure what play that character is in.

Head size: 42 inches (106 cm) thick

Famous Swine
Unwilling to be typecast, Link steers clear of "Pigs in Space" fan conventions. Which is easy, because there haven't been any.

I'M READY FOR MY CLOSE-UP.

Hat Head
Link thinks he looks good in hats (especially when he can't find his toupee). In fact, he picks his projects by the hats that go with them.

Jacket size: 44 inches (112 cm) long

MUPPET FILE
Debut
The Muppet Show #203
Talents Looking handsome
Training
North Hollywood School for Hams

Lips

Lips was a late addition to the Electric Mayhem band when the guys realized they needed a brass instrument and a sixth member with whom to divide their expenses. Lips has played with the group on and off for years.

Has a major problem with split-ends.

Music Schooled
When not playing with The Electric Mayhem, Lips serves as a guest lecturer at the Susquehanna School of Music and Hat Making on Bagel Street.

Never been seen with his eyes open.

Fugue-et About It!
Lips has received numerous offers to put out his own line of signature trumpets. He has repeatedly declined—it's all about the music for him.

Cool Vibrato
Lips started taking trumpet lessons when he was in elementary school. He got his nickname when on a cold day he decided to practice outside and got his lips stuck to his horn.

HOW 'BOUT A LITTLE TRAVELIN' MUSIC!

His favorite trumpet—all his others are at the pawnshop.

MUPPET FILE
Debut
The Muppet Show #501
Special Talent Puckering
Favorite Key
C-sharp

Lobsters

The earliest Muppet lobsters arrived on the scene courtesy of the Swedish Chef. They were originally purchased as an entrée, but when Kermit saw their potential as entertainers, they were replaced on the menu by tasty, but less talented peanut butter and jelly sandwiches.

Rock Lobsters
When promoted from dinner to rock band members, the lobsters' agent renegotiated their contract and they moved out of their pot and into a real dressing room.

Bad Polly
In *Muppet Treasure Island*, Long John Silver traded his traditional parrot in for Polly Lobster (or Bad Polly). Apparently feathers make Long John ticklish.

MUPPET FILE
Debut
The Muppet Show #209
Dislikes Melted butter
Special Talent Turning red when blushing or boiling

Lost claw in a fight.

POLLY WANT A BIGGER PART IN THE MOVIE

Thinks his claw makes his hook look tiny.

The Muppet Theater

The Muppet Theater is the long-time performing home of The Muppets. Constructed in the early 20th century by Benny Vandergast for his famous "Vandergast All-Monkey Follies of 1927," the theater went into disrepair when the popularity of all-simian vaudeville revues waned. J.P. Grosse won the theater at a poker game, and when he couldn't decide whether to use a wrecking ball or bulldozers to tear it down, he rented it out to Kermit the Frog.

The Muppets' house band in the orchestra pit.

Balcony Hecklers
The house-right balcony box is always reserved for Statler and Waldorf. They've been there so long that there are some who believe the theater was constructed around them.

HI-HO, EVERYONE!

Where The Audience Sits
The audience seats are upholstered in comfy red velvet. This photo was taken during a performance by Fozzie Bear. Apparently, the entire audience thought it was a good time to get refreshments.

IS IT TIME TO MEET THE MUPPETS?

PLAY MUSIC! LIGHT LIGHTS!

J.P. Grosse—
he owns the place.

Backstage

No matter what kind of craziness was happening onstage at the Muppet Theater, it was always a sure bet that there was even more craziness happening backstage. Host, producer, and director Kermit the Frog worked tirelessly to assemble a show from the assorted nonsense he had at his disposal. Upstairs from Kermit's home base are several dressing rooms—including one for Miss Piggy and one devoted to the week's guest star.

Exit (for everyone except the Flying Zucchini Brothers. They leave by blasting themselves through the roof.)

The Stage Door
To enter the theater, guest stars passed through the stage door and through an airtight security system: an oft-dozing doorman named Pops. Pops' unbeatable identification procedure for visitors consisted of a simple but probing "Who are you?"

Miss Piggy's dressing room—enter at your own risk.

State-of-the-art sound system

Not sure what this is, but it's probably rented.

Dressing room for snakes

Fire bucket. Oddly, it's the only thing that's ever caught fire.

Louis Kazagger

Louis Kazagger is the primary (and only) correspondent for the Muppet Sports Channel. Confident Kazagger brings fans the events they never knew they were missing (and wish they had missed after seeing)—from cross-country billiards to goldfish shooting and everything in between.

> WHAT'S YOUR FAVORITE OLYMPIC SPORT?

> SYNCHRONIZED HECKLING.

Bullseye!
Kazagger commentated on the archery competition during the Muppets' version of Robin Hood. His coverage was cut short when a practice arrow went astray, but he recovered quickly!

> WE HAVE A WINNER... AND WE NEED A STRETCHER!

Holds several records for continuous sports-related speaking.

Sporting Life
Kazagger originally wanted to pursue a career in law, but developed a taste for unusual sports when he happened to attend a cheese hurling tournament and was hit in the face with a camembert.

Made from an old couch.

MUPPET FILE
Debut
The Muppet Show #308
Favorite Sport Wig racing
Least Favorite Sport
Bagpipe eating

Lubbock Lou's Jughuggers

Jugheads

Lubbock Lou dreamed of playing in a symphony orchestra, but none of them required a jaw harp player. He formed the Jughuggers when he was stuck with an empty jug after failing to get a deposit back.

Juggling Jugbands

The Jughuggers joined the Muppets after the Gogolala Jubilee Jugband split following a dispute over putting a hole in a washtub.

Gramps
The band's fiddle player is named Gramps. Oddly, he has no grandchildren and thinks they are calling him "Cramps."

Slim Wilson
Guitar player Slim Wilson joined the Jughuggers after his first group, Slim and the Sheep Dippers, broke up.

Gramps fiddles on the fiddle.

Bubba plays the jug.

"The Other" Lou—the band's only female singer

Slim Wilson on guitar

Zeke on the banjo

MUPPET FILE

Debut
The Muppet Show #211

Likes Barn dances, hoedowns, shindigs

Dislikes
Hullabaloos

Luncheon Counter Monster

Like many Muppet monsters, Luncheon Counter Monster has a voracious appetite for—well, basically, anything. Maintaining a balanced diet, he eats fruit for vitamins, trees for fiber, flatware for iron, and some of his co-stars for protein.

HE LOOKS MEAN. I'LL STAY AWAY FROM HIM.

HOW ABOUT WE JUST STAY AWAY FROM ALL THE MUPPETS?

Had horns sanded down after an unfortunate incident at the barbershop.

Hold the Mayo
Some believe Luncheon Counter Monster got his name from where he sat in his debut. The truth is he got it because he likes to eat luncheon counters—mainly those with gravy stains.

Hunger Games
Luncheon Counter Monster's omnivorous nature made it hard for him to make friends at school and even harder to not eat them.

99% of his thoughts are eating related. 1% are about modern art.

RRRRRRAH!

MUPPET FILE
Debut
The Muppet Show #206
Likes Carbohydrates
Dislikes
All other hydrates

Lydia the Pig

When Kermit decided to sing the classic tune "Lydia the Tattooed Lady," he arranged an open casting call for someone to dance the title role. By coincidence, a tattooed pig named Lydia showed up. Miss Piggy thought it was a little too much of a coincidence.

DO YOU HAVE ANY TATTOOS?

NOPE. I PREFER TO BE THE ONE DOING THE NEEDLING.

Pretty as a Picture
Lydia's tattoo of Andrew Jackson actually looks more like Andrew Lloyd Webber. Her tattoo artist reimbursed her for that one.

Color not found in nature

Popular Pig
Lydia ended her debut by showering Kermit with kisses. She was a smash hit, but made only a few other appearances. Miss Piggy may have had something to do with that.

ANYBODY KNOW A GOOD TATTOO REMOVAL GUY?

Tattoos were done by Maury James.

MUPPET FILE
Debut
The Muppet Show #102
Likes Mazurka dancing
Favorite Tattoo
Washington Crossing the Delaware

115

Veterinarian's Hospital

Veterinarian's Hospital features Rowlf as Dr. Bob, and Miss Piggy and Janice as two nurses who aren't smart enough to hide behind assumed names. In this madcap medical facility, patients lose patience waiting for cures amidst a barrage of gags, and the audience is often in intensive care, wishing for a case of amnesia.

It's a Gas!
It doesn't help the home audience, but Dr. Bob makes his jokes funnier in the operating room by using a generous supply of laughing gas. The crew has to hurry to complete the show before it wears off.

HAS THE PATIENT RECEIVED HER ANESTHESIA, DR. BOB?

Dr. Who?

A quack who has gone to the dogs, Dr. Bob received his medical training from reading the instructions on a box of adhesive bandages. His comedy training was acquired by reading cartoons in bubblegum packaging.

OH YES! SHE WON'T BE WAKING UP FOR SOME TIME, WILL SHE, NURSE JANICE?

I'M SURE OF IT!

Mad Monty

Although best known as a bloodthirsty pirate, Mad Monty is really a pussycat. (Actually, we're not exactly sure what he is underneath his matted mop of fur, but "pussycat" is as good a guess as any.) When he isn't buccaneering, Monty enjoys embroidering clever sayings on dainty pillows.

WHAT MAKES MONTY SO MAD?

HE HASN'T FIGURED OUT A WAY TO ESCAPE FROM THIS BOOK!

Keeps a spare hat under this one.

Pulling The Wool Over His Eyes

Mad Monty developed his unique look at an early age when his mom helped him put on his hat with a little too much force.

Method Actor

While making *Muppet Treasure Island*, Monty stayed in character. He even tried to take over the makeup trailer and sail it to the Caribbean.

Hasn't had a haircut in 16 years.

Carefully selects hatbands that don't clash with his eyes.

MUPPET FILE

Debut *Muppet Treasure Island*

Special talents Timber shivering, plank walking, swashbuckling

Dislikes People who draw little happy faces

Mahna Mahna and the Snowths

Mahna Mahna is a vocalist of few words. Just two, in fact. This ultra-hip scat-singer and percussionist has his own backing group—the Snowths. What exactly are Snowths? Ask them and all you'll hear is: "Doo-doo-do-doo-doot."

Signature Song

Mahna Mahna and the Snowths have performed their signature song "Mahna Mahna" on TV shows, in commercials, live theater and the film *The Muppets*.

MUPPET FILE

Debut
The Ed Sullivan Show

Special talents
Popping up out of nowhere

Mahna-mian Rhapsody
Mahna Mahna and the Snowths appeared in Bohemian Rhapsody, substituting their own usual lyrics for the originals—and making no more sense than the originals.

If the eyes are the windows to the soul, Mahna Mahna's soul could be very dark indeed.

Round snouts make for excellent vowel sounds.

Mama Fiama

The doting mother of Johnny Fiama, Mama Fiama arrived in America as a small girl. Mama enjoys nothing more than reminiscing about her childhood in the old country—even though she doesn't remember exactly which old country she came from.

What's Cooking?
Mama Fiama can usually be found cooking a pot of sauce. She has been fine-tuning her recipe since the Eisenhower administration. The secret ingredient? Love (and oregano).

Keeps secret pasta sauce recipe under her hat.

Loses glasses even when she's wearing them.

One Tough Mama
She may seem like a helpless little old lady, but Mama Fiama can wield a mean frying pan and rolling pin in self defense (or in a pre-emptive strike).

I MAKE-A THE SAUCE!

MUPPET FILE
Debut
Muppets Tonight #102

Special Talent
Making sauce

Favorite Restaurant
Johnny Fiama's Pasta Playhouse

Marvin Suggs and his Muppaphone

Marvin Suggs has a flare for music, showmanship, and inflicting pain. But Marvin doesn't inflict pain for fun. It's all in the interest of art—the art of pounding tune after tune on his living (and aching) musical instrument, the Muppaphone.

Absence of Mallets

Marvin invented the Muppaphone by accident. He tripped and fell on a little fuzzy creature, whose shriek of pain proved to be a perfect G note.

Shirt purchased from Flamenco Fred's Ruffle-rama.

Gavel Banger

In the "Alice in Wonderland" episode of *The Muppet Show*, Marvin presided as judge. Using his gavel, he pounded the jury instead of the Muppaphone.

MUPPET FILE

Debut *The Muppet Show* #105

Hometown Somewhere in France

Pet Peeve Members of the Muppaphone going flat

OW!!!

ANOTHER DAY, ANOTHER HEADACHE.

Mean Mama

Mean Mama was discovered when she was waiting tables in a truck stop in Plaster City, California. After a successful tour she joined Kermit's troupe. She managed to eat only four trucks on tour, impressing everyone.

Palate Cleanser

With a long career as a lovable yet menacing presence, Mean Mama has retired from show business for now. If the young monsters don't have what it takes, she's ready to step in.

> I'M SORRY, MISS, BUT THESE SEATS ARE TAKEN

> I THINK SHE'S GOING TO TAKE THEM ANYWAY

Someone once said that her eyes were bigger than her stomach. We know this not to be true.

MUPPET FILE

Debut
The Muppet Show #201
Likes Trips to the beauty parlor
Dislikes
Insincere people—they taste bitter

This tooth is actually a cap. She broke it while biting into a frozen dinner that she didn't heat up.

> RRRAAARGH!

The technical word for this tooth is "stalagmite."

Mildred Huxtetter

A **warm and** endearing woman with a colorful frock, a curly mop of hair, and a sparkly pair of glasses, Mildred enjoys music and dancing. She has temporarily left show business to follow her dream of creating a line of designer cheese knives.

MUPPET FILE

Debut The Muppets Valentine Show pilot

Education BA, MA, Ph.D., O.B.E., and R.S.V.P.

Seeking True love and the ultimate muumuu

> SOME GIRLS HAVE ALL THE LUCK... I'M NOT ONE OF THEM.

Know-It-All
Mildred prides herself on her knowing all the answers. These aren't necessarily the answers to the questions being asked, but they are still answers.

Mildred has 20/20 vision, but thinks she looks better with glasses.

Looking for Love
Mildred wears her heart on her very frilly sleeve and hopes to find Mr. Right someday. (At this point, she'll settle for Mr. Wrong or any other Mr. that happens to be available).

123

The Moopets

Appearing nightly in the Pechoolo Casino in Reno, the Moopets are a tribute band who rip off the Muppets and exploit their fan base. While the Muppets are bright and optimistic, the Moopets are dark and cynical, turning Kermit's classic song "Rainbow Connection" into a cheesy hotel jingle.

Roll Call
Fozzie Bear himself played with the group in *The Muppets* movie, but he was replaced by a lookalike when he left to rejoin the original Muppets. Animool recently left the group to pursue a solo career and asked us not to include him in this picture.

Used to work as a Britney Spears impersonator.

Apparently, all bears wear hats.

FOR REALLY.

WHAT THE WOCKA...

HI-HO, YOURSELF.

WHAT ARE YOU LOOKING AT?

Name: Foozie
Role: Bogus Bear

Name: Kermoot
Role: Fake Frog

Name: Miss Poogy
Role: Sham Superstar

Name: Janooce
Role: Mock Musician

Name: Roowlf
Role: Pretend Pooch

Obedience school dropout

I DON'T HAVE A CATCHPHRASE.

125

Ebony, Ivory, and Pork
In *Muppets Most Wanted*, Miss Piggy performs a star turn on a grand piano. The diva viewed pianos in 28 different colors to find one that went with her dress.

Miss Mousey

Miss Mousey is a sweet and demure mouse who performed from time to time on *The Muppet Show*. A classically trained Shakespearean actor, she met Kermit the Frog when he came to see a performance of *Mouse Ado About Nothing*. Afterwards, Kermit offered her a job.

STATLER, THERE'S A MOUSE IN MY COFFEE.

NOT SO LOUD. EVERYBODY WILL WANT ONE.

Froggy Affections
In her first appearance, Miss Mousey was the target of Kermit's affections. Fortunately for her (and Kermit), this was before Miss Piggy joined the Muppets. Miss Piggy is still wary of Miss Mousey.

Never removes bonnet—some believe she's losing fur on top.

Only uses mascara tested on humans.

Sorority Mouse
Miss Mousey left the Muppets quite some time ago (at the gentle suggestion of a certain pig). She now teaches theater classes in a small college in Wisconsin.

MUPPET FILE
Debut *The Muppets Valentine Show* pilot

Favorite Board Game Mousetrap

Least Favorite Object Mousetrap

ACTUALLY, I PREFER MS. MOUSEY.

Miss Piggy

Miss Piggy is the porcine queen of the Muppets. Raised on a small farm, she is now a starlet and commanding presence. But actually her bravado and aggressive karate kick mask a sensitive soul who wants the love of her fans and her frog.

Entre le Entourage
While Miss Piggy loves being a superstar, it is hard work—it takes hours to read the résumés of all the people she hires to do everything for her.

Piggy considers this her best side.

Casual, windblown look requires four hours of styling.

Animal Magnetism
Miss Piggy has adored Kermit for more than three decades. While Kermit prefers to keep his feelings private, Piggy wants everyone to know how she feels about her frog.

Haughty Couture
Miss Piggy had a very difficult upbringing on the farm and wore the same dress every day. That may be the reason she is so obsessed with her wardrobe today.

KISSY-KISSY!

MUPPET FILE
Debut Herb Alpert and the Tijuana Brass

Special talents Martial arts, bon-bon eating

Dislikes Fresh air

Likes Times Square

Favorite Food Whaddaya got?

Fashion and Moi

Kissy-kissy! Moi, Miss Piggy has been given two measly pages to write about moi's approach to fashion. Moi doesn't just approach fashion. Moi runs right up to fashion and yells "Here Moi Am!" Enjoy just a few of moi's favorite & fabulous looks...

This hair took four hours—moi hopes you appreciate it.

Pearls go with everything—and so does moi.

Animal prints are all faux—some of moi's best friends are animals.

Well Suited
A crisp white suit is the perfect thing to wear for a day of shopping for crisp white suits—or for the endless photoshoot during which this très adorable picture was taken.

People say moi's ears are moi's best feature. Personally, moi loves them all!

The ultimate accessory— a pair of gorgeous eyes.

Yes, it's real. But, don't look too close.

A diva is judged by the height of her heels, not the depth of her heart.

Bouncy and Flouncy
Black with a splash of pink is the kind of bold look that has made moi a fashion icon! Moi must thank some of moi's many designers: Calista, Babs, Polly, and Stephen—and moi am sure they thank moi for making their work look so good.

Catch of the Day
A fishtail dress is a strong statement that only certain figures can make. Fortunately, moi's is one of them. Rich tones like this one accentuates moi's creamy complexion and makes it even more striking than usual.

Mulch

Mulch grew up in an idyllic suburban home in Boonton, New Jersey, with his sister, Composta Heap. They moved there from Eastern Europe as part of a monster relocation program. After being teased for his resemblance to movie monsters, Mulch decided to capitalize on this and go into show business.

Me and my 'Goyle
Mulch's favorite role was Quasimodo in *The Hunchback of Notre Dame*. He hopes to one day play his other dream role—Death in *Death of a Salesman*.

Head hinges open to allow easy brain access.

Nose doesn't work well. How does he smell? Pretty bad.

I LOVE DEBBIE HARRY!

Monster Match
After several appearances in monster movies and an unfulfilling day job as a barista, Mulch eventually found steady work as assistant to Dr. Phil Van Neuter on "Tales from the Vet".

MUPPET FILE

Debut
The Muppet Show #509

Special Talent Scaring his own reflection

Likes
Butterflies

Dislikes
Caterpillars

Muppy

Muppy is a cute dog with an unkempt mop of fur and a bad attitude. Unlike many other Muppet dogs, Muppy does not seem to speak. Nobody is sure if he can't speak, or if he's just holding out for a better contract.

Mega Biter
While it is said of many dogs that their bark is worse than their bite, the same cannot be said of Muppy, who has a tendency to bite guest stars, co-stars, and often a certain frog.

Bad Dog! Bad Dog!
Kermit puts up with Muppy only because the dog's biggest fan is J.P. Grosse, the owner of the Muppet Theater.

Muppy usually communicates through Scooter.

WOOF!

Muppy has slightly shaggier fur than Rufus.

Debut
The Muppet Show #101
Special Talent Negotiation
Dislikes Constantly being mistaken for Rufus
MUPPET FILE

Mutations

The Mutations are a bizarre dance crew that appeared throughout the entire run of *The Muppet Show*. Joining guest stars in a musical performance, the Mutations really made a name for themselves.

Step Out of Time

After their initial contract expired, the Mutations spent three decades hosting a dance-based competition show. They finally rejoined Kermit's band of entertainers in time to appear in the gang's 2011 feature film.

It's Time To Meet the Mutations

The Mutations helped to recreate *The Muppet Show* opening in the film *The Muppets*. Just as in the original version, only two out of the three Mutations participate.

This guy dyes his fur to match the others.

YOU'RE BOTH OUT OF STEP!

Takes two hours to pull pants over enormous furry feet.

MUPPET FILE

Debut *The Muppet Show* #102

Likes Individuality

Dislikes Rainy days and Mondays

The Newsman

The **Muppet News** division has only one correspondent, known to all as The Newsman. Incessantly interrupting the action with his breaking news reports, he usually bears the brunt of breaking news—by getting broken. He often doesn't make it to the end of a broadcast...

Eyewitless News

The Newsman received his degree from the Ralph J. Murrow School of Journalism and Frozen Foods, where he majored in hard news and soft ice cream.

Hair combed carefully to appear journalistically tousled.

Eyebrows grew back after being singed.

Wears glasses to look serious.

MUPPET FILE

Debut
The Muppet Show #102

Special Talent
He heals quickly

Likes
Human interest stories

Dislikes
Hard-hitting journalism

Weighty News Story

When things started falling on him from above, the Newsman asked that the Muppet Newsroom be moved. It didn't help. Nothing can restrict the press or the laws of gravity.

Good Night and Good BOOM!

The Newsman was nominated for an award for his report on the sudden incidents of reporters blowing up. He accepted the award upon his release from the hospital.

HERE IS A MUPPET NEWS FLASH!

Nigel

Nigel's first job was host of one of the pilots for *The Muppet Show*. His shy manner lost him the job when the series went into production. Kermit felt bad about Nigel's dismissal, and gave him a new assignment as orchestra conductor.

MUPPET FILE

Debut *The Muppet Show* pilot

Special talents Transposing, arranging, and waving a stick

Training Tommy Newsom Academy of Music & Charisma

Heavy eyelids make him susceptible to hypnotism.

In The Pits
Nigel returned to the pit to conduct the orchestra for the Muppet Telethon in the 2011 film, *The Muppets*. Nothing much had changed—even that tuna sandwich he left was still there.

Impossible to figure out where Nigel's face ends and nose begins.

Themes Like Old Times
Nigel conducted and wrote the catchy theme song for *The Muppet Show*. Floyd Pepper thinks the song is very uncool.

I'M HIP. NO, REALLY— I'M HIP.

Nigel

A TV director must remain calm and cool at all times. The *Muppets Tonight* budget couldn't afford someone like that, so they got Nigel instead. Frantic, crazed, and panicky, Nigel called all the shots in the control room, or, to be more accurate, he screamed them.

On the Air
After *Muppets Tonight*, Nigel gave up television directing and took up a career with considerably less stress and strain—he became an air traffic controller.

Brain never stops directing. His dreams look terrific.

Nigel never blinks —TV directors don't.

Seeing Double
Nigel bears a resemblance to Droop, a glum little guy first seen in *The Muppets Valentine Show* pilot. They may share a silhouette, but their personalities are like night and day.

Requires very powerful inhalers for asthma attacks.

TAKE ONE! NO! TAKE TWO! TAKE TWO!

MUPPET FILE

Debut *Muppets Tonight*

Training Peter Harris TV Academy— Elstree Campus

Dislikes Ulcers

Monsters

Muppet monsters come in all shapes, sizes, and degrees of hunger. Many are friendly and docile, others live by a simple code: "Meet, Greet, Eat, and Repeat." Whether furry, feathered, scaled, or completely indescribable, these guys are always unpredictable. It's advisable to use extreme caution when approaching monsters, and extreme speed when running away from them.

Chopped Liver
An alien from the far away planet Zabar (located on the Upper West Side of the Andromeda Galaxy), Chopped Liver was a frequent foe of the *Swinetrek* crew on "Pigs in Space."

The Snerfs
With necks that stretch and contract to the beat and large green feet that love to dance, it's not surprising that the Snerfs' natural habitat is the musical production number.

Horn noses usually tuned to b-flat

Hugga Wugga
Hugga Wugga first came to Earth in 1971 with an extended visit to a Las Vegas show. His nose-horn emits bursts of steam—which is useful for repelling foes and steaming clothes.

Enjoys a diet high in omega-6 fatty acids for a shiny coat.

Fern and Anthony

As seen on MuppeTelevision's "Hurting Something," Fern and Anthony are just an average married monster couple. They deal with the same problems that everyone does—balancing home life with work, dealing with emotions, and deciding what kind of wine to drink when eating people.

The Vile Bunch

These wicked beasts earned the name "The Vile Bunch," when they helped a rock star on his quest for souls at the Muppet Theater. After much soul searching, they gave up and opened a frozen custard stand near Devil's Tower, Wyoming.

I'M HIDEOUS! ISN'T THAT WONDERFUL?

Silver Beak has his face polished once a week.

Beakie was once nominated for a Fred Award for Best Unexplainable Creature.

Bad disposition caused by sinus trouble

Old Tom, Dead Tom, Real Old Tom

Old Tom, Dead Tom, and Real Old Tom are three pirates who sailed the bounding main in *Muppet Treasure Island*. They are actors, and the only piracy they are guilty of happens during contract negotiation.

Three Toms, no waiting

Old Tom
Old Tom doesn't like being called "Old Tom." He prefers being called "Old Thomas." During the holiday season, Old Tom makes extra cash playing Santa Claus in department stores that have very low standards.

Dead Tom
Many have wondered how a dead pirate got to serve on the *Hispaniola*, but the answer is simple—they knew he wouldn't eat much.

Real Old Tom
Real Old Tom is not as old as he looks. In fact, he's older! His real name is Really, Really, Real Old Tom and he underwent four hours of makeup each day to look younger. His actual appearance is closer to that of Dead Tom.

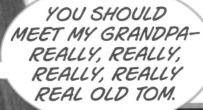

YOU SHOULD MEET MY GRANDPA— REALLY, REALLY, REALLY, REALLY REAL OLD TOM.

MUPPET FILES

OLD TOM
Debut
Muppet Treasure Island
Likes
Pillaging at his own pace
Dislikes
Whippersnappers

DEAD TOM
Debut
Muppet Treasure Island
Favorite Song "Dry Bones"
Dislikes
Lying perfectly still

REAL OLD TOM
Debut
Muppet Treasure Island
Likes
Golden Girls reruns
Dislikes
Osteoporosis

Paul Revere

MUPPET FILE

Debut
The Muppet Show #221

Likes Show tunes

Dislikes Glue

Show Business is actually Paul Revere's second career. He was previously involved in horse racing—oddly enough as a jockey. He gave it up after several horses complained. His comic timing was discovered by Kermit at a horse show and Paul Revere soon had a new job.

Suffers from dry, flyaway mane.

Has his teeth whitened regularly—it's easier than having his fur darkened.

YEAH, I TALK. WHAT'S THE BIG DEAL?

Shoe Business
After leaving horseracing, Paul Revere traded his horseshoes for sneakers. They're more comfortable to wear, but he does need help tying the laces.

The Horse Right Here
Paul Revere received his name when he appeared in a performance of Frank Loesser's "Fugue for Tinhorns" from *Guys and Dolls*. He prefers the music of Cole Porter.

141

Pig on the Half Shell
The opening song of *Muppets Most Wanted* features a spectacular appearance by Miss Piggy in a clamshell precariously positioned over a pool of water. What do you think happens next?

Penguins

> WATCH YOUR MOUTH, BUSTER!

If you had the choice of living in the bitter cold of the Southern Hemisphere, or working in a comfortable studio, you'd pick the studio, right? So did the Muppet Penguins, and their happiness is reflected in the unbridled joy with which they entertain.

> Penguins are a girl's best friend.

> WHAAAAAAACK!

The Penguin March
While their favorite musical style may be the march, they are also accomplished purveyors of show tunes, rock, big band music, and cool jazz. (When the Penguins play it, it's cold jazz.)

Band of Brothers
Penguins naturally tend to gather in groups—which explains the ease with which they work together in large production numbers and musical combos.

The penguins like to wear tuxedos on top of their natural tuxedos.

MUPPET FILE
Debut
The Muppet Show #304
Likes Old Sushi
Dislikes
Global Warming

Pepé the King Prawn

The greatest Spanish export since Antonio Banderas, offshore Malaga native Pepe has brought a zest for life and a spicy attitude to the Muppets. Pepe is adored by fans and friends, even though they may not always understand what he's saying.

Prancing Prawn
A gifted dancer, Pepe planned to perform a number with Miss Piggy in *The Muppets*, but when a lift went wrong he was left feeling flat.

Hot and Spicy
Pepe considers himself a "Ladies Prawn," and is often seen in the company of a beautiful "womens"—as he would say.

> I AM NOT A SHRIMP! I AM A KING PRAWN, OKAY?

Double Act
Pepe made his debut in a comedy team with Seymour the Elephant. Hoping to find humor in their size difference, Pepe instead found himself frequently being crushed.

Only buys irregular clothes because he needs four sleeves.

MUPPET FILE

Debut
Muppets Tonight #102

Full Name Pepino Rodrigo Serrano Gonzales...Etcetera

Likes Salsa (the dance, not the condiment)

Dislikes Scampi

Mr. Poodlepants

He's bubbly—he's whimsical—he's indescribable—he's Mr. Poodlepants! No one knows exactly what brought Mr. P. to the Muppets, but this first-rate chucklehead with a passion for silliness has taken time off to write his autobiography, *They Call Me Poodlepants*.

Coast to Coast Host

Mr. Poodlepants and his puppet, Clownie, have taken their children's show to many TV stations. He usually gets cancelled after only a few episodes, but hey—there are lots and lots of TV stations out there.

Uses immersion blender to style hair.

Doesn't need glasses, but wears them for looks.

Murder on the Disoriented Express

Mr. Poodlepants cast silliness aside long enough to play the victim in an Agatha Christie sketch. It turned out that the real victims were the members of the audience.

The most understated jacket in his closet

> *WHOO-HOO! I'M THE KING OF TWIRLY-WOO!!*

MUPPET FILE
Debut Muppets Tonight #101
Likes Pants
Dislikes Poodles

Pigs

Pigs are reliable members of the Muppet ensemble. They show up for work on time, they don't complain a lot, and they're not picky eaters—which is a good thing when the Swedish Chef is in charge of catering. The pigs made their first appearance in the pilot for *The Muppet Show* and have been wallowing around with the Muppets ever since.

Honolulu of a Luau
Many members of the Muppet pig ensemble hail from Hawaii, and grew up enjoying sun and fun on the beach while trying to avoid overenthusiastic luau chefs.

AND TO FINISH EL PYRAMIDO, I GO ON TOP!

The Bouncing Borcellino Brothers
This troupe of acrobats from Boston made only one disastrous appearance on *The Muppet Show*, plummeting through the stage during their "El Pyramido" routine. They're now practicing for a second shot. No one has the heart to tell them the show isn't in production.

SHOULDN'T SOMEONE BE STEERING THE SHIP?

Hoping to finally get a promotion

Joined the crew by pretending to be a very tiny pig.

Pigs in Space

The undisputed stars of "Pigs in Space" are Link Hogthrob, First Mate Piggy, and Dr. Strangepork, but a crew of 25 toil away alongside them on the spaceship *Swinetrek*. As in other "trekking" TV space shows, we only see a few crewpigs at a time.

WHY DOES TINY GO ON TOP? HE'S 975 POUNDS!

Pillage Idiots

The male pig ensemble performed "In the Navy" as a horde of Vikings who invade a quiet village. Their leader, Link Hogthrob, descends from real Vikings (including "Link the Cowardly Mediocre," who was known more for hiding and cowering than plundering and pillaging).

147

Pops

Pops is the stage doorman at the Muppet Theater. He has show business in his blood (it got there when he got a splinter from the stage in his foot). Forgetful Pops is not very sharp and observant, and he has a tendency to fall asleep in mid-sentence.

> *IT'S GOOD TO SEE SOMEONE OUR AGE.*

> *I DIDN'T THINK ANYONE OUR AGE WAS STILL AROUND!*

Checking In
In *The Great Muppet Caper*, Pops ran the front desk of the Happiness Hotel. He was happy that Kermit made him work behind the desk, because he often forgets to put on his pants.

Pops' eyeglasses are as thick as they can be while still being transparent.

Sweet Tooth
Although many think Pops received his nickname because of his old age, he has actually been called Pops since childhood. His name was inspired by his fondness for lollipops.

> *WHO ARE YOU?*

MUPPET FILE
Debut
The Muppet Show #501
Special Talents Napping, snoozing, dozing
Likes
To not be bothered

Prairie Dog Glee Club

The cutest kleptomaniacs ever to hail from the dusty trails of the American West, this pack of prairie dogs harmonizes vocally and steals locally. Some psychologists believe they just want attention, but these rodent rascals really just want the stuff they're stealing—because it's shiny.

Laying Down the Law

Kermit has a zero-tolerance policy when it comes to crime backstage. But, despite his warnings, the Prairie Dog Glee Club continued to steal the show—and everything else in the theater.

Bear Facts

These little guys may be innocent-faced and furry, but they'll steal anything they can get their sticky little paws on, as Patrol Bear and his chief discovered in "Bear on Patrol."

MUPPET FILE

Debut
The Muppet Show #322

Favorite Stolen Item
Kermit's mug

Favorite Sentence
5 to 10 years

LISTEN GANG, IT'S NOT NICE TO TAKE PEOPLE'S THINGS...

NICE COLLAR YOU HAVE THERE, KERMIT.

Kermit's collar is about to be swiped. He usually keeps a spare in his locker.

Quongo

As a baby gorilla, Quongo dreamed of a life away from the mountains—little did he know how far from the mountains he would end up. His show business experience includes singing, dancing, and throwing coconuts. In his spare time, he wrestles professionally.

Gorillas have large brains, so Quongo has trouble finding hats that fit.

MUPPET FILE

Debut *The Muppet Show* #219

Likes Bananas

Dislikes People who assume he likes bananas

King Quong

Like another well-known gorilla, Quongo has scaled skyscrapers. But, in his case, it's only because he has a dreadful fear of elevators.

Keeps fur short to make him look younger.

Career Aspirations

While he enjoys his work, Quongo sometimes gets frustrated at being typecast. He would really love to do more dramatic roles. There are only so many ways you can throw a coconut.

OOOOH-OOOOH-AHHH-AHHH!

Rizzo is a clever huckster with a soft heart, an aggressive attitude, and an endless appetite. Rizzo is always working an angle, running off-the-books backstage tours and attempting to sell ads in this book—which we put a stop to.

The Rat Pack
Rizzo is the unofficial leader of the Muppet rat community, mostly because of his ability to avoid traps and successfully navigate mazes.

Can hear a whisper from 20 yards (18 meters) away. 30, if the whisper is food-related.

Now, Try the Pest
Rizzo considered opening a chain of fast-casual eateries called "Rizzo's Ratskeller," but health code regulations barring rats from restaurants would have prevented him from visiting his own establishment.

WHEN DO WE BREAK FOR LUNCH?

AND DINNER, FOR THAT MATTER.

MUPPET FILE
Debut
The Muppet Show #418
Likes
Any kind of food
Dislikes
Running out of food

151

Rats

With the possible exception of the docks of New York City, nowhere will you find a larger collection of vermin than in the Muppets. Unlike the ones found in New York, the Muppet Rats display a wide range of talents, abilities, and wardrobe.

GIMME AN R!

Cheer Up!
The rats' energy and enthusiasm make cheerleading a good outlet for them, but not many engage in the sport. After all, they are hard to see from even the front rows—and then there's also the risk of trampling.

Saddle shoes from Shelly's Shoe Shack & Cheesery

The Rat in the Hat

CHEEEEEESE!

Take it From the Bottom
Rats are good dancers—this probably comes from years of scurrying. The biggest challenges for rat dancers are a lack of jobs and the risk of being stepped on during tap dance finales.

Egyptian rat in a loincloth.

Rizzo and the Ratpack
In his earlier days, Rizzo led a rock band. However, after a successful tour of American sewers, the group split when something came between them— a disagreement over how to divide up a pizza.

THE LONG AND WINDING RODENT...

Work Hard, Play Harder
The rats' favorite part of their job is vacation, and they love seeing the world—although at their height, everywhere looks pretty much the same.

Jazzy Hawaiian shirt tells everyone he's a tourist.

NO THANKS, I'VE GOT POPCORN.

153

Robin

Kermit the Frog has approximately 2,353 siblings, so the chances of other talented frogs showing up are high, and his nephew Robin proves that. Robin loves performing and enjoys being a member of Frog Scout pack no.12.

The Frog Prince
Robin made his first splash in *The Frog Prince*. He hid his connection to Kermit, but it's obvious to anyone that the little guy's talent is what got him the job.

Long and Short of It
The diminutive Robin and the humongous Sweetums have found an uncommon friendship because of their common trait—being a different size than nearly everyone else.

MUPPET FILE
Debut *The Frog Prince*

Likes Traveling in the overhead compartment

Dislikes Being tripped over

Contrary to rumor, his eyes are not ping-pong balls, they just look like them.

Little Frog, Big Dreams
Robin admires and idolizes Kermit and is already following in his uncle's flipper-steps. The little guy's recording of "Halfway Down the Stairs" made the UK top ten.

Does tongue exercises to improve fly eating ability.

Voted fastest flippers in his Frog Scout troop.

FOR MY NEXT NUMBER... SEVEN

Rowlf

After his first burst of superstardom waned, Rowlf concentrated on his music and his fleas, making a comeback on *The Muppet Show* and becoming beloved by fans as "the dog who plays the piano."

Roll Over Beethoven
Rowlf's performance of Beethoven is very moving—it moved a bust of the late composer to complain. Even so, Rowlf continues to play *Moonlight Sonata* in broad daylight.

I AIN'T NOTHIN' BUT A HOUND DOG!

Ears are so sensitive, he can hear music even when the radio is off.

Lights! Camera! Fetch!
A showbiz vet (who goes to a showbiz vet), Rowlf ran the camera in *The Muppet Movie*. After three takes, he put some film in it.

Chasing a Schtik
When not working on his music, Rowlf played Dr. Bob in Veterinarian's Hospital—the only medical show where only the jokes were in need of first aid.

MUPPET FILE

Debut
Purina Dog Food Commercial

Favorite Composers
Woofgang Amadeus Mozart, Johann Sebastian Bark

First Album Recorded
Ol' Brown Ears is Back

Canine Composer
Rowlf is a key part of the Muppets orchestra but often performs solo. His performance style is very animated, with his ears seemingly keeping rhythm.

Rufus

Rufus is a cute, cuddly, lovable, and very large Muppet dog. Not only is he man's best friend, but he's *everybody's* best friend. He is loyal, helpful, and incredibly energetic. He has a wide range of talents and abilities (or at least he thinks he does).

THAT RUFUS IS A PRETTY SMART DOG.

IF HE'S SO SMART, WHAT'S HE DOING HERE?

Light On His Paws
Rufus once signed up for a dance class, but left prematurely when the instructor wanted to charge him extra for his second pair of legs.

Rufus loves props, such as hats, steering wheels...

Speak! Speak!
An endearing presence, Rufus may not be able to speak like Rowlf and some other Muppet dogs, but he can still get his message across—if he's communicating with someone who is good at charades.

Applied for a job as a bloodhound, but he can't stand the sight of blood.

Could use a breath mint right about now.

HAAAAAAH!

Debut The Land of Tinkerdee
Likes Ear scratching
Dislikes Being mistaken for Muppy

MUPPET FILE

Sal Monella

Best known as Johnny Fiama's assistant, chauffeur, valet, and bodyguard, Sal grew up on the lower east side of a South American rain forest and relocated to the US as a child. He dropped out of school when he learned he was never actually enrolled.

Chimp On His Shoulder

Sal is loud, obnoxious, abrasive, coarse, and annoying. He has his softer side, though we have yet to see evidence of it.

JOHNNY FIAMA COMING THROUGH!

Johnny Fever

Sal is completely devoted to his boss, Johnny Fiama. Despite Johnny's occasional money problems, Sal has stuck by his side—even though he hasn't been paid for more than 72 weeks.

Sal is buying a three-piece suit one piece at a time.

MUPPET FILE

Debut *Muppets Tonight* #102

Likes Mama Fiama's pasta sauce

Dislikes Fans who crowd Johnny

159

Sam Eagle

Sam is the Muppets' self-appointed censor, moral compass, and all-around party pooper. If there are any hijinx going on, Sam will take it upon himself to shut them down. He is rarely successful.

Say Uncle, Sam

As a bald eagle, Sam represents all things American. He has a collection of 917 American flag lapel pins, but seldom wears clothing into which he can pin them.

If You Can't Beat 'Em

After years of attempted censorship and pointless editorials, finally Sam joined in the nonsense, taking serious roles in *The Muppet Christmas Carol* and *Muppet Treasure Island*.

Sam is considering getting a toupee.

Eyebrows grew together when Sam was just an eaglet.

YOU ARE ALL WEIRDOS!

MUPPET FILE

Debut
The Muppet Show pilot

Likes All things American

Dislikes American flags that are made in other countries

Scooter

Scooter got to where he is by doing the things no one else wanted to do (it also helped that his uncle owned the Muppet Theater). He's smart, eager, and enthusiastic. Scooter is now stage manager.

Eyeglasses by I've Been Framed, Ltd.

Simon Smith Says
Scooter sometimes steps into the spotlight. He and Fozzie performed *Simon Smith and his Amazing Dancing Bear*. Fozzie played the bear.

Pickin' and Grinnin'
Scooter has been practicing playing his guitar for quite some time and demonstrated his ability with Six String Orchestra.

TEN MINUTES TILL SHOWTIME!

New Media Mogul
Scooter enjoyed a brief career with a large internet company. Hint: it starts with the letter "G" and rhymes with "zoogle."

Flashing his "Sure, Boss, anything you need!" smile.

The Muppet Show crew jacket is his prized possession.

MUPPET FILE

Debut *The Muppet Show* #101

Special Talents
Knocking on doors, being cheerful

Secret Dream
To be a super action hero

161

Under the Sea

Something's **often fishy** with the Muppets—and it's not just the featured performers in Lew Zeland's act. Many varieties of undersea life have found their way into Muppet productions. Since most Muppet productions are produced on dry land, their stories are literal "fish out of water" tales.

A Peek at Pike
Walleye Pike was one of the members of the crew in *Muppet Treasure Island*. He was the only pirate who actually looked forward to walking the plank.

HAVING FUN?

WE ALWAYS HAVE A WHALE OF A TIME!

A Whale of a Tail
Kermit and Robin helped whales Molly and little Melville avoid a boatful of whaling (but not wailing) pigs in an episode of *The Muppet Show*.

HURRY UP, WE'RE LATE FOR SCHOOL!

Good as Gold
Though much larger than typical goldfish, these fine-finned friends swam their way through several appearances of *The Muppet Show*. They had outstanding musical ability—after all, they did have scales.

WE WON'T BE AROUND FOR AN ENCORE!

Want Some Seafood, Mama?
"Hold Tight, Hold Tight" featured a veritable aquarium of sea life and one piano-playing dog. A trio of singing fish, plus a shark joined a lobster for the number.

Eight is Enough
With eight tentacles making his bass playing four times better than most musicians, this Muppet Octopus had plenty of free time to tend to his shady garden.

Seymour

This prodigious pachyderm initially ran the elevator at the K-MUP television studio with Pepé the King Prawn. Eventually they got their break on camera. Seymour has returned to the elevator business, which has its ups and downs.

Custom hat made from enough fabric to make 17 regular-sized hats

Always keeps his trunk packed.

Two of a Kind
When Seymour and Pepe had enough of elevator work, they took a job running the K-MUP canteen. This caused the entire cast and crew of *Muppets Tonight* to lose their appetites and eat out.

Two of a Kind
Seymour has a positive and large personality. He is proud of his generously proportioned profile and has included a tribute to his "big behind" into his and Pepe's theme song.

GOING UP?

MUPPET FILE
Debut
Muppets Tonight #102
Likes Peanut brittle
Dislikes
Compact cars

Sopwith the Camel

Sopwith is a Bactrian camel—he has four legs, two humps, and one heck of a talent for dancing. While most Bactrian camels live in Asia, Sopwith has a condo in Arizona, which he shares with his girlfriend, whom he met on camelmatch.com.

I DON'T CARE WHAT ANYONE SAYS, I'M THIRSTY

MUPPET FILE

Debut *The Muppet Show* #313

Favorite Desert Gobi

Favorite Dessert Chocolate cake

Favorite Day Wednesday

Desert Flyer

Sopwith got his name from the World War I-era biplane, the Sopwith Camel. Although named after the plane, Sopwith the Camel is actually afraid of flying and prefers romantic strolls in the moonlight.

If camels have calves, do calves have camels?

Big feet prevent him from sinking in sand—and also from wearing sneakers.

Moving Right Along

One of Sopwith's biggest roles has never been shown. He was filmed carrying Statler and Waldorf for *The Muppet Movie* but the scene ended up on the cutting room floor.

Spa'am

Wears large headdress in an effort to make himself look slimmer.

He named the skull on his headdress "Fred."

Tried to sell spear on internet.

In *Muppet Treasure Island*, the title island is home to a native tribe, the high priest of which is Spa'am, a surly boar with an evil eye and a large appetite.

MUPPET FILE
Debut *Muppet Treasure Island*
Likes Having his tusks polished
Ironic Fact When traveling, Spa'am orders the kosher meal

What a Boar!
To overcome the myth that boars are bores, they threw a party for cast and crew, but forgot to invite anyone. So, while they are no longer considered boring, they are still considered stupid.

SILENCE, SMELLY SAILOR MANS! YOU HAVE VIOLATED SACRED ISLAND.

Not-so-Fine Print
The character Spa'am is not related in any way to any other person, animal, character, hologram, vehicle, place, or canned luncheon meat. (Our lawyers made us put this in—we have no idea why.)

Splurge

Before there was Thog, before there was Sweetums, there was Splurge—a monster who is big on size, small on words. Although cast for his huge size, he always hoped to someday have a role that would not involve him breaking something or crashing through a wall.

> THAT GUY REALLY BRINGS DOWN THE HOUSE.

> AND EVERY OTHER BUILDING IN THE VICINITY.

Needs help to scratch his head—his arms can't reach.

Enjoys chewing gum—300 sticks at a time.

Who Was That Masked Monster?
In "Hey Cinderella," Splurge demonstrated his expertise in the art of disguise. With his mask on, he is almost impossible to recognize.

Stomach rumblings can be heard from the neighboring town.

Walking Tall
Splurge was the first huge creature Kermit hired to join the Muppets. The frog was tired of climbing a ladder to change light bulbs in the office. Unfortunately, Splurge wasn't much help—his arms are incredibly short.

> I'M SITTING HERE TO SHOW SCALE.

MUPPET FILE
Debut *Cinderella* 1965 pilot
Likes Radishes
Dislikes Flying coach

167

Pigs in Space

Captain Link Hogthrob, First Mate Piggy, and Dr. Julius Strangepork lead the spaceship *S.S. Swinetrek*, exploring the universe and boldly going where no swine has gone before—making sure they are always **home in time for dinner!**

OH SHUT UP, BACON BRAIN!

Swinetrek Cockpit
Whether you call it the bridge, the cockpit, or the place where the main pigs sit, the control room of the *Swinetrek* is the ship's nerve center. From this one room, all major systems of the ship can be controlled—except for the parts that are uncontrollable... or just plain difficult.

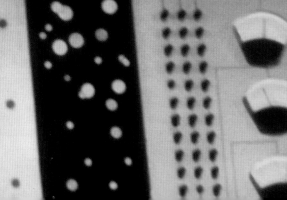

OH, THE ENDLESS SAMENESS OF ETERNAL SPACE!

SIGH

S.S. Swinetrek
The *Swinetrek* is a WhenPigsFly-class spacecraft, which is capable of near-light-speed and around-the-clock meal service.

Star Boars
One of the villains that the *Swinetrek's* crew encountered was the "icky" Dearth Nadir. Nadir battles his enemies and has a nasty case of asthma.

A Giant Leap for Pigkind
Captain Hogthrob and Dr. Strangepork will stop at nothing to discover the vast mysteries of space—or at least why socks disappear from the dryer.

Statler

One half of the greatest team of professional hecklers in show business history, Statler is enjoying a second career, having retired from his Wall Street job. Many believe Statler single-handedly caused the Great Depression by endlessly criticizing every single investor.

Making a Scene

On occasion, Statler and Waldorf play film roles, such as the Marley brothers in *The Muppet Christmas Carol.* But even when in character they still speak their minds— especially when a certain bear is involved.

Cleft chin inherited from great-grandfather, along with a measly $3.

> THIS BETTER BE GOOD. AWW, WHO AM I KIDDING?

Seating Derangement

For years, Waldorf was seated screen left with Statler at screen right. They switched places after Statler won this heated game of "Odds and Evens."

MUPPET FILE

Debut
The Muppet Show pilot
Likes Very little
Dislikes
Almost everything

Carp Ad Nauseum

The duo have always enjoyed heckling bad television shows at home. With the advent of new media, they are now able to heckle webisodes, mobisodes, and any other "-isode" they can find, too.

The Swedish Chef

A culinary master of questionable abilities, the Swedish Chef has been a Muppet mainstay since answering an ad placed by Kermit seeking a part-time cook who could speak—and cook—gibberish. The Chef's specialty? Hard to swallow but hilarious recipes.

Hat can also be used to strain pasta.

Service with a Smile
After serving meatballs with a tennis racket, the Chef was smacked with a fine by both the International Tennis Society and the World Culinary Club.

Luck of the Irish?
The Chef enjoys singing Irish music with Animal and Beaker. Their version of "Danny Boy" brings a tear to the eye (and a queasiness to the stomach). But hey, it's better than eating his food.

BØRK, BØRK, BØRK

Vertical stripes are slimming.

Swede Dreams
When viewers noticed that the Chef did not speak real Swedish—or any other known language—Kermit sent him for language lessons. He studied French, majoring in toast and minoring in fries.

MUPPET FILE
Debut
The Muppet Show pilot

Favorite Dish The onewith the happy face painted on the bottom

Training
Are you kidding?

Muppet Food

From the pantry to the proscenium, Muppet food has a long tradition of entertainment and nutrition, but some of their antics are a bit hard to swallow. The one thing unhappy audiences have yet to figure out is what to throw at food after bad performances.

Fake eyebrows. Giant carrots don't grow facial hair.

PRESENTING... THE CARROTS OF PENZANCE

DOES THIS HAT MAKE ME LOOK FATTENING?

Dancing Fromage
Under the direction of François Fromage, the dancing cheeses have proved to be a great addition to the Muppet food lineup—until the lights get too hot and they melt.

Seven-Foot-Tall Talking Carrot
A masterful performer of light opera, the carrot arrived because Kermit misunderstood a request for a seven-foot talking parrot.

Has more beta carotene in his feet than most opera singers have in their whole bodies.

173

Sweetums

Sweetums is a tall, furry ogre whose forbidding appearance belies his lovable nature. He has a surprisingly large fan following among the teen demographic. Sweetums shrugs off the attention, enjoying his work too much to concentrate on stardom.

Eyebags are larger than most ladies' purses.

Helping Hands
Backstage, Sweetums is in demand for reaching high places and lifting heavy things. Well, he did list those tasks on the special skills section of his acting resume.

Car Jack
Between acting jobs, Sweetums helps out at Mad Man Mooney & Son's Used Car Lot. He easily regains his fitness when he returns to the Muppets, as he is always trying to catch up with their car.

Big and Small
Since co-starring in *The Frog Prince*, Sweetums and Robin have become close friends. The only downside to their friendship is the risk of some kind of sitting-related accident.

MUPPET FILE
Debut *The Frog Prince*
Likes Breakfast, lunch, dinner (he's not much of a dessert person)
Dislikes Clothes shopping

Talking Houses

There goes the neighborhood! Four talking houses inflicted a series of groan-worthy gags on each other (and the audience) in the first season of *The Muppet Show*. They left show business when the other houses on their street threatened to relocate if the jokes didn't stop.

WHAT DO YOU THINK OF THESE HOUSES?

I THINK THEY SHOULD BE CONDEMNED.

MUPPET FILE

Debut
The Muppet Show #104

Special Talents
Providing shelter, keeping out rain

Dislikes Tight siding, loose windows, housepainters with a heavy hand

Home Improvement
While these particular talking houses were introduced on *The Muppet Show*, an earlier talkative abode appeared in a series of commercials in the 1960s.

DID I TELL YOU ABOUT MY SON, THE HOSPITAL?

I HEAR YOU'RE COMING DOWN WITH SHINGLES.

BIG DEAL. MY KID'S A BANK.

NO, I SAID MY SHINGLES HAVE BEEN COMING DOWN.

Thog

Though originally on the villain's side in *The Great Santa Claus Switch*, Thog proved to be a lovable guy whose heart is as big as the rest of him (and that's pretty big). His sweet personality and gentle manner have won him many fans.

Thog's Big Break
A couple of years ago, Thog tired of squeezing through the tiny stage doors and hitting his head on the lights. He took a long break at his ranch, relaxing on a heavily reinforced hammock.

Fallen Arches
When "Big Blue" returned for the 2011 film *The Muppets*, he found that either he got bigger or *The Muppet Show* arches got smaller. He didn't quite fit through them any more.

Earthshaking
Thog was a keen jogger until several seismic research facilities begged him to stop. His running measured 6.5 on the Richter Scale.

MUPPET FILE
Debut The Great Santa Claus Switch
Likes Flowers, sunsets, cars with lots of headroom
Dislikes Diets, low doorways

Timmy Monster

Timmy was born to perform. At an early age, he could be found dancing on the kitchen table (and the table could be found in pieces on the floor). After honing his skills in school talent shows and local amateur nights, Timmy was granted an audition for The Muppets. He got the job!

MUPPET FILE
Debut *The Muppet Show* #117
Special Talents Eating large portions
Favorite Food He's not picky

Furry Footwork
Timmy was featured in several major Muppets musical numbers. Although he didn't exactly have flying feet, fans agreed that he was a natural. (A natural what? Nobody knows.)

He has his mother's eyes (and she wants them back).

A Koozebanian Phoob hitches a ride.

Leaving the Stage
After his stint with the Muppets, Timmy pursued a career on Broadway. Despite good reviews (his "Curly" in *Oklahoma* received raves), he never made it to the top. Timmy retired from show business and now runs a small organic bakery called "Timmy's Treats."

Muppets on Wheels

Since leaving their home and the comforts of the Muppet Theater, the gang has relied heavily on a variety of modes of transport to get from place to place. While the Muppets usually arrive at their destination, the same can't always be said about their vehicles.

Station Wagon

This wood-paneled Ford station wagon was marked down from $1,195 to $11.95. Sweetums squashed a fly onto the price tag, adding a decimal point. Not one of Mad Man Mooney's best cars, it broke down in the middle of the desert.

Electric Mayhem Bus

This psychedelic school bus has been The Electric Mayhem's main transport for years. After its debut in *The Muppet Movie*, the bus returned in *Muppets From Space* and had a brief, dilapidated cameo in *The Muppets*.

Purchased his first bicycle from Orville Wright, famous inventor.

Tire needs inflation.

Car in Disguise

Repainted in a rainbow-colored disguise, Fozzie's uncle's Studebaker gave Kermit and Fozzie their first lift in T*he Muppet Movie*. It now resides in the Studebaker National Museum.

Kermit and Fozzie behind the wheel again.

Minimum Maximum

Seen in *Muppets Most Wanted*, the Le Maximum belongs to Interpol agent Jean Pierre Napoleon. The vehicle was one of the largest European cars on the market until it became illegal throughout most of Europe for its immense size.

Hoping his cool musician friends don't see him.

Has no idea he's on a bicycle right now.

Hates getting fur caught in the chain.

Trying to think up some big, dangerous finish to this ride.

Bicycle buddies

After Kermit's bike solo in *The Muppet Movie*, the rest of the gang all wanted to get in on the two-wheeled fun.

Uncle Deadly

Uncle Deadly is a veteran actor who trod the boards of the Muppet Theater long ago. Hurt by a bad review, he hid in the recesses of the theater, emerging years later to haunt the Muppets as the Phantom of the Muppet Show. He later joined them as resident spooky creature.

MUPPET FILE

Debut: *The Muppet Show* #119
Special Talents: Haunting
Likes: Spooky sound effects
Dislikes: Critics

He is considering plastic surgery— to add more wrinkles.

Has his teeth cleaned every 26 years.

Dastardly Muttering

Always playing the villain, Uncle Deadly puts the drama into melodrama with his evil English accent and slow, creepy delivery.

Alas Poor Deadly

Uncle Deadly's performance in *Othello* received the worst reviews in the history of acting. This was probably because he had mistakenly memorized the script for *King Lear*.

MWAH-HA-HA-HA-HA!!!

Brand new clothing dragged through parking lot to look old.

Say Uncle, Uncle

Uncle Deadly was so excited that part of *The Muppets* movie was made on the same stage as the classic film *The Phantom of the Opera* that he struggled to stay in character.

Waldorf

Waldorf and his cohort in criticism, Statler, built their fame by tearing down others. So, why does he make the effort to leave his home to see every single thing the Muppets do? If you don't know, then you've never met his wife, Astoria.

Bah! Humbug!
Waldorf joined Statler to play Jacob and Robert Marley in *The Muppet Christmas Carol*. They didn't much care for the rest of the movie.

Queen Astoria
Waldorf has been married to Astoria for so long that he can't recall where they met. It wasn't love at first sight, but he did find her face strangely familiar.

Purposely doesn't put battery in hearing aid.

Suspender Sentence
Waldorf came to heckling after selling his business—a clothing shop for lawyers called Law Suits While You Wait. Each suit came with a temporary restraining order.

MY FOOT'S ASLEEP... WISH I WAS TOO.

MUPPET FILE

Debut *The Muppet Show* pilot

Special Talent Finding something bad to say about anyone

Pet Peeve There's not enough room to list them all

Walter

When production began on *The Muppets*, Walter, one of the Muppets' biggest fans, wrote a letter to the producers. This resulted in a screen test for a character named Walter. In one fateful moment, he went from Muppet fan to Muppet.

Part of the Family
Officially a member of the Muppets, Walter appeared in *Muppets Most Wanted*. He learned that being a Muppet isn't so much fun when it was his turn to take Animal for a walk.

Needs a haircut... just this one hair.

Put Your Lips Together and Blow
In addition to his almost annoying optimism, Walter has an incredible musical talent—a whistle that rivals that of a nightingale.

When his whistling made him famous, Walter considered getting his mouth insured.

Trick or Treat
For years, Walter has been dressing up as Kermit the Frog for Halloween. Next year, Kermit is thinking of dressing up as Walter just to mess with him.

MUPPET FILE
Debut *The Muppets*

Special Talent Whistling

Wants Dr. Teeth variant Action Figure

I HAVE THE BEST LIFE IN THE WHOLE WORLD!

Muppet Madness

Walter still gets very excited when he is included in photos with the Muppets. In fact, when he discovers he is in this encyclopedia, he'll totally freak out. Walter! Walter! Snap out of it, Walter! If anyone reading this is near Walter, splash some water on his face.

The Whatnots

In addition to all of the characters we know and love, there's a group of unsung, unheralded, and often unnamed performers who populate the world of the Muppets—the Whatnots. With a simple change of costume, hair and facial features, they can play a variety of characters.

Whatnots can change age and gender in minutes.

Whatnots work a variety of occupations—which means they have to join a lot of unions.

Eyes of all shapes and sizes make whatnots (and trash bags) come to life.

PLASTIC?

OR PAPER?

Plentiful accessories help Whatnots develop unique personalities— and shopping addictions.

TIME FOR A Q+A. I'LL START WITH THE "Q."

Some Whatnots wear very dark sunglasses so you can't see that they don't have eyeballs.

Wigs, beards, and loincloths make time travel possible. Anyone for clubbing?

MAN, IT'S DARK IN HERE! I WISH I HAD EYES.

Props like musical instruments help round out the character and fill out the band.

Wanda

Wanda, along with Wayne form the singing duo "Wayne and Wanda." A favorite of Sam Eagle, this wholesome couple start with a song and end up all wrong. Their tendency to end up battered and beaten made it hard for them to get noticed for musical excellence.

Wears steel liner in hat "just in case."

Uses fireproof shampoo.

Sign Language
Wayne and Wanda first met at a music store. They were waiting for a sign that they should team up when a big sign shaped like a piano fell on them.

AH, SWEET MYSTERY OF LIFE...

Long, full skirt makes walking and singing more dangerous.

Refraining From The Refrain
Wayne and Wanda's inability to complete a performance may have been why Kermit did not rehire the duo after the first season of *The Muppet Show*.

MUPPET FILE
Debut The Muppet Show #101
Biggest Fan Sam Eagle
Relationship Status It's complicated

Wayne

Wayne is the other half of the team of Wayne and Wanda. With a crisp tenor voice, he would be a major singing star—if he could only reach the second verse. His place is beside Wanda—usually inside the local hospital.

Dislocated shoulder in 1978. It still hasn't been relocated.

...AT LAST I'VE FOUND THEE!

Secret Coda
Kermit recently rehired Wayne and Wanda. They hope to someday finish a performance. They've started actually learning the endings to their songs.

Half Note
Wayne enjoys studying magic as a hobby. He tried to put it to use during a performance of "You Do Something to Me." This was their only performance in which something other than the song was cut short.

MUPPET FILE
Debut The Muppet Show #102
Special Talent
Perfect pitch (in baseball, not singing)
Relationship Status
Whatever Wanda said

Woodland Creatures

The **still of** the wilderness is sometimes interrupted by the sounds of nature: grunts, squeaks, squawks, and—when the Woodland Creatures are around—beautiful music. Foxes, raccoons, opossums, beavers, and rabbits are among the animals populating some of the most memorable Muppets musical numbers.

Masked Marvels
Raccoons may look like they wear masks, but it's just their fur colors. They only really wear masks when engaging in their hobby—dressing up in costumes.

Pop Music
The Woodland Creatures sometimes play instruments constructed from items discarded in the forest. The fox hopes that one day someone will throw away a xylophone.

Hates playing possum. Prefers checkers.

Man Smart, Critter Smarter
Some of the animals' best performances have a strong message—the need to preserve our natural environment. This is a bit ironic since many of them have moved to condos in the city.

HIYA, POSSUM

IT'S O'POSSUM. I'M IRISH.

MUPPET FILE
Debut *The Muppet Show*
Dislikes Hunters
Likes Gatherers

Zelda Rose

Not much is known about Zelda Rose, and she's not happy about that. She has been trying to break into show business for years, but has mostly been stuck doing background work. Zelda's not giving up, though. Between jobs, she waits in the audience, ready to jump to the stage in an emergency.

Wears hair barrette to cover a bald spot.

Has worn the same shade of eye shadow for 40 years.

Shhhhhhh!

When not performing, Zelda works as a librarian. Since she is always rehearsing, she is, in fact, the only librarian whose patrons tell *her* to be quiet.

Big Break

Zelda thought she hit the big time with her act "Zelda Rose and Her Singing Owl." But they only performed once—the owl quit when Zelda refused to give up top billing.

Nose was once mistaken for a snack cake.

WHO?

MUPPET FILE

Debut
The Muppet Show pilot

Special Talent
Alphabeticization

Favorite Dewey Decimal Number
791.45/72

Zoot

One of the founding members of The Electric Mayhem, Zoot is a musical genius, but when not playing, he seems to be a little out of sync with the rest of the world. He can often be found backstage curled up on a sofa or chair grabbing a few extra Zs.

Zoot of all Trades
In his dreams, Zoot plays every instrument in the band. He works harder asleep than he does when he is awake.

Still owes three payments on his sax to Erickson's House of Horns

Few Words
Although his sax licks are loquacious, Zoot himself doesn't do a lot of talking. When he does speak, it's usually something incredibly profound like "Huh? What?"

Blue Zoot
Zoot likes his bandmates and has vowed to never leave the Electric Mayhem—probably because his solo album, "Zoot Plays The Blues," sold just six copies.

Wears sandals so his toes can feel the music

MUPPET FILE
Debut The Muppet Show pilot
Likes Blues
Dislikes Travelers

Index

Index

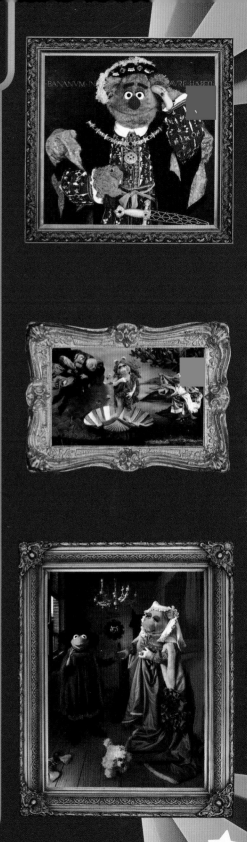

DK

LONDON, NEW YORK, MUNICH,
MELBOURNE, AND DELHI

Senior Editor Victoria Taylor
Editors Julia March, Zoë Hedges
Editorial Assistant Lauren Nesworthy
Senior Designers Lisa Robb, Guy Harvey,
Robert Perry, Lynne Moulding
Designers Nick Avery, Alison Gardner
Managing Editor Laura Gilbert
Design Manager Maxine Pedliham
Publishing Manager Julie Ferris
Art Director Lisa Lanzarini
Publishing Director Simon Beecroft
Pre-production Producer Rebecca Fallowfield
Producer Danielle Smith

First published in the United States in 2014 by
DK Publishing
4th Floor, 345 Hudson Street, New York 10014

14 15 16 17 10 9 8 7 6 5 4 3 2 1
001-253450-Feb-14

Page design copyright
©2013 Dorling Kindersley Limited

Published in Great Britain by
Dorling Kindersley Limited.

A catalog record for this book
is available from the Library of Congress.

ISBN: 978-1-4654-1748-0

Color reproduction by AltaImage
Printed and bound in China by South China

ACKNOWLEDGMENTS

DK would like to thank the author Craig Semin and consultant
Jim Lewis for their expertise and Muppetational humor.
We would also like to thank Chelsea Alon, Jessica Ward,
Scott Phiel, Ryan Ferguson, Roxanna Ashton, Rachel Alor,
Betsy Mercer, Catherine Bridge, Debbie McClellan,
Jessica Bardwil, Dale Kennedy, Dominique Flynn,
Tracy Gilbert, Jeffrey Sotomayor and Caitlin Dodson at Disney.

Discover more at
www.dk.com